STANISLAVSKI

FOR BEGINNERS™

DAVID ALLEN

ILLUSTRATED BY JEFF FALLOW

Writers and Readers Publishing, Inc.
P.O. Box 461, Village Station
New York, NY 10014

Writers and Readers Limited
35 Britannia Row
London N1 8QH
Tel: 0171 226 3377
Fax: 0171 359 1454
e-mail: begin@writersandreaders.com

Text Copyright © 1999 David Allen
Illustrations Copyright © 1999 Jeff Fallow
Cover Design: Paul Gordon
Book Design: Emma Byrne

A Writers and Readers Documentary Comic Book
Copyright © 1999
ISBN # 0-86316-268-1 Trade
1 2 3 4 5 6 7 8 9

Printed in Finland by WS Bookwell

Beginners Documentary Comic Books are published by Writers and Readers Publishing, Inc. Its trademark, consisting of the words "For Beginners, Writers and Readers Documentary Comic Books" and the Writers and Readers logo, is registered in the U. S. Patent and Trademark Office and in other countries.

Writers and Readers

publishing FOR BEGINNERS™ books continuously since 1975

1975:Cuba • 1976: Marx • 1977: Lenin • 1978: Nuclear Power • 1979: Einstein • Freud • 1980: Mao • Trotsky • 1981: Capitalism • 1982: Darwin • Economics • French Revolution • Marx's Kapital • Food • Ecology • 1983: DNA • Ireland • 1984: London • Peace • Medicine • Orwell • Reagan • Nicaragua • Black History • 1985: Marx Diary • 1986: Zen • Psychiatry • Reich • Socialism • Computers • Brecht • Elvis • 1988: Architecture • Sex • JFK • Virginia Woolf • 1990: Nietzsche • Plato • Malcolm X • Judaism • 1991: WWII • Erotica • African History • 1992: Philosophy • • Rainforests • Miles Davis • Islam • Pan Africanism • 1993: Black Women • Arabs and Israel • 1994: Babies • Foucault • Heidegger • Hemingway • Classical Music • 1995: Jazz • Jewish Holocaust • Health Care • Domestic Violence • Sartre • United Nations • Black Holocaust • Black Panthers • Martial Arts • History of Clowns • 1996: Opera • Biology • Saussure • UNICEF • Kierkegaard • Addiction & Recovery • I Ching • Buddha • Derrida • Chomsky • McLuhan • Jung • 1997: Lacan • Shakespeare • Structuralism • Che • 1998: Fanon • Adler • Marilyn • Cinema • Postmodernism

Contents:

DAVID ALLEN,
AUTHOR

JEFF FALLOW,
ILLUSTRATOR

David Allen teaches drama at the University of Wolverhampton. He has contributed to a variety of publications such as the INTERNATIONAL DICTIONARY OF THE THEATRE and NEW THEATRE QUARTERLY. He is the author of PERFORMING CHEKHOV (published by Routledge).

Jeff Fallow is a freelance illustrator and graphic designer living in Fife. He is also author and illustrator of the forthcoming **Scotland for Beginners**™, and **Wales for Beginners**™ and a political cartoonist, with work published in CND TODAY and SCOTS INDEPENDENT.

Stanislavski revolutionised our ideas about acting.
His discoveries still form the basis of actor training in the Western theatre. But they have often been misinterpreted, and some important aspects of his work remain little known.

The Stanislavski "system" emerged from his own practice and struggles as an actor and a director. He never saw it as a rigid set of rules for an actor to follow; indeed, his ideas and methods were continually changing and developing. He wrote,

My system is the result of lifelong searches... I have tried to find a method of work for actors to enable them to create the image of a character, breathe into it the inner life of a human spirit, and, through natural means, embody it on stage in a beautiful, artistic form. The foundations for this method were my inquiries into the nature of an actor.

Stanislavski's "lifelong searches" into the nature of acting began when he was some seven years old and he was playing Winter in a family entertainment about the Four Seasons. The boy felt acutely self-conscious: he did not know where to look, or what he had to do.

What's my motivation in this scene?

He had been given a stick and told to mime putting it into the flame of a candle. "Remember, it is only make-believe," the others told him. Stanislavski decided to do it for real.

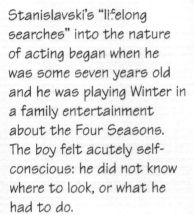

It seemed a completely natural and logical action to me.

Of course, it started a real fire..

Looking back, Stanislavski said that the experience taught him the importance of having a purpose and a meaning in all your actions on the stage, and how awkward you feel when these are missing.

But it can surely only have been with the benefit of hindsight that Stanislavski could see so much significance in this episode. Either that or he was a very bright seven-year-old...

Stanislavski was born in Moscow, on January 5, 1863, the son of a rich textile manufacturer. He was baptised Konstantin Sergeyevich Alekseyev; "Stanislavski" was a stage-name he adopted later. The theatre, the circus and the opera fascinated him from an early age. At home, he created his own little circus troupe, calling it "Konstanzo Alekseyev's Circus." Brothers, sisters and friends performed as acrobats, clowns, and even horses. Stanislavski was the director, and grabbed the best parts. His eldest brother, Vladimir, who played the music, did not take it seriously. In the middle of a performance, he would stop everything, and lie on the floor.

I don't want to play any more!

The performance was spoiled; all its **"reality"** was lost. "And that was the most important thing for us," Stanislavski said.

It was necessary to believe it was all serious and real - or it wasn't interesting.

He gave up his circus, and started a puppet theatre, complete with trap door and stage lights. He recreated dramatic scenes and spectacular effects from plays he had seen, as realistically as the cardboard scenery would allow. In one production the fire was so real, the scenery burned down... This was becoming a habit! The love of creating realistic and dramatic stage effects never quite left Stanislavski...

When Stanislavski was 14, his father turned a wing of their country house into a theatre. The first production was an evening of one-act plays. For his part in a piece called A Cup of Tea, Stanislavski simply copied the work of an actor he admired - reproducing his moves and gestures and even his voice. The day of the performance arrived.

At last, I was on the stage, where I felt wonderful. Something exciting and inspiring inside me seemed to be driving me on, and I flew through the whole play... I thought I was a great artist, putting on a show for the admiration of the crowd.

Unfortunately, the audience didn't agree. He acted at such speed that no one understood a word he said ...

Stanislavski's family formed its own amateur theatre group, the **"Alekseyev Circle."** Over the next few years, he played many roles, mostly in vaudevilles and skits and light operettas. He kept a journal about his performances and was relentlessly self-critical. It seemed as if the harder he tried, the more the audience criticised him for overacting.

He concluded that excitement was not enough - he must learn the value of restraint and control, what he called "a feeling of true measure."

In 1881, he spent the summer preparing two one-act comedies, trying to find this "feeling of true measure." Visitors, invited to watch rehearsals, fell asleep from boredom.

It's good, but rather - quiet.

YAWN

So, the actors spoke louder. Then spectators complained they were shouting. One visitor said that speed was important in a light comedy. Stanislavski decided to cut the running time.

The Act takes forty minutes... When it takes twenty minutes, it will be perfect.

At last, it seemed they were playing at the right speed and volume. But then the same visitor told them,

I don't understand anything you're saying, or anything you've doing. You're running about like a group of madmen.

So they tried again...

The work was painful, but it produced results. The actors "began to speak more distinctly and to act more definitely." But looking back, years later, Stanislavski saw that there was no "inner life" to the performances. It was speed for the sake of speed; technique for the sake of technique.

And when that's the case, there can be no feeling of truth.

When not acting in plays, members of the Alekseyev Circle enjoyed dressing up as beggars, drunkards, or gypsies, and going down to the train station, where they would frighten people. They had to be as convincing as possible.

In real life, it was necessary to perform with more truthfulness than on stage - or we could get into trouble. We must have played our parts well, since we were chased away.

Whilst rehearsing a play called A *Practical Man* (1883), the company decided to live their roles throughout the day. Whether they were walking in the garden or taking a meal, they had to stay in character, and act according to the play's given circumstances. It was a significant development. Stanislavski began to feel he was really "living" the role, rather than simply showing off.

But he was upset when some young ladies told him, after the performance,

It's such a pity you're so ugly!

The young Stanislavski became driven by a passion to seem dashing and handsome on the stage. He loved to appear in thigh-length boots, with a sword and a cloak.

Vanity, he later said, was leading him away from the path of true art.

It became one of Stanislavski's basic principles: "Love the art in yourself, not yourself in art."

He was tall -over six foot - and notoriously clumsy. When he walked into a room, people hurried to remove anything breakable in case he knocked it over. Stanislavski worked tirelessly, almost obsessively, to improve his voice, his movement and gestures, watching himself in a mirror - a practice he later condemned.

PAH!

It is dangerous to use a mirror. It teaches the actor to look at himself from the outside, rather than looking inside.

He continued to copy other actors he had seen. This was a common practice; indeed many drama teachers actively encouraged it.

But the imitation of a favourite actor can only create an external method, and not the inner soul.

He felt acutely the absence of any system or method to his acting. In 1885, he began to study acting at a drama school, but left after three weeks. The teachers, he complained, were very good at showing students the results they should aim for...

BLAH BLAH

But nothing was said about how to do it, what method and means to use to achieve the desired result.

There was no **system**.

SALVINI AS OTHELLO

Stanislavski claimed he learnt most by watching great actors. He saw the Italian tragedian **Tomasso Salvini** play *Othello* in 1882. On his first entrance, Salvini did not look impressive: he wore a very obvious wig, and his costume made him look fat. Nevertheless, he soon held the audience transfixed. For Stanislavski, the performance was a model of powerful, clear, and truthful acting. All great actors like Salvini seemed to have something in common. Stanislavski sensed this, but he could not explain it. What was it? What was the secret of great acting?

I racked my brains, but I could not find the answer.

The famous Russian actor, **Mikhail Shchepkin** (1788 - 1863), had died the year Stanislavski was born, but his influence on the theatre remained. He introduced a new, realistic style of acting. He declared: "Take your models from life" - not from the stage. Stanislavski tried to read everything Shchepkin had written...

"Always have nature before your eyes. Get under the skin of your character..."

"You might sometimes act badly, sometimes only satisfactorily (it often depends on your inner mood), but you should always act truthfully."

"It is much easier to play everything mechanically, for nothing is required except reason... But an actor of feeling - that's something else again."

M. S. SHCHEPKIN

Perhaps influenced by Shchepkin, Stanislavski moved away from copying other actors, to find his models in real life. In a French operetta, Hervé's *Lili*, for example, he felt he found the movement, speech, and tempo of a typical Frenchman. This was a "success in a way, for if I did imitate, it was not a ready-made, empty stage model, but something living, something I myself had observed in real life." He was still concentrating on the **externals** of the role, however - working from the outside in.

It is possible to arrive at the internal by way of the external. This, of course, is not the best, but nevertheless it is one possible way-in to creative work. And it helped me now and again to live my part.

He was slowly learning to become an *"actor of feeling"*.

The Alekseyev Circle was one of the best amateur groups in Moscow. Months of preparation went in to every production. In 1887, Stanislavski produced *The Mikado*. The production demonstrated his growing skill as a master of theatrical spectacle. It included some dazzling effects, especially in the crowd scenes.

There was a kaleidoscope of continually changing and moving groups, and fans of every size, colour and description swept rhythmically through the air, in time to the music. It was the Alekseyev Circle's crowning achievement; after that the company began to break up. Stanislavski's sisters, brothers and friends had grown up and were going their separate ways.

In 1888, the group performed for the last time. Stanislavski continued to perform, appearing in amateur productions wherever and whenever he could. The performances were thrown together hastily, and most of the actors seemed more interested in gossiping, flirting and drinking, than in serious work.

Stanislavski was not deterred.

What could I do? There were no other places to act, and I was absolutely dying to act.

However, he was concerned about his position in society so he decided to take a stage name. By day, he was Konstantin Alekseyev, working for the family firm. At night, he became "Stanislavski," appearing in amateur theatres throughout Moscow. He kept his double life a secret, even from his parents. But one night they surprised him by turning up at a performance of a risque French farce. The next day his father scolded him.

If you are determined to act in your free time, start a proper drama circle with a decent repertoire, but don't appear in filth like that with God knows who.

In 1888, **The Society of Art and Literature** was born.

FYODOR KOMISSARZHEVSKI

Joining Stanislavski to create the new Society were...the opera singer, Fyodor Komissarzhevski

...and the professional theatre director, Aleksandr Fedotov

They planned to form a club to bring together artists of all kinds. Stanislavski invested his own money to obtain the premises, and restore them to a fit state.

ALEKSANDR FEDOTOV

The first play performed (on 8 December 1888) was Pushkin's *The Miserly Knight* - with Stanislavski as the knight. In the play, a medieval baron descends at night into the cellar of a tower where his riches are hidden. He gloats over his money and power but then remembers that death will take everything away. He howls with despair. Fedotov saw the character as a pitiful old man, dressed like a beggar.

But Stanislavski had different ideas...

I was already beginning to see myself as a copy of a well-known Italian baritone, with his well-shaped legs in black tights... and most importantly, a sword!

When he told the director and designer how he wanted to play the part, they just laughed.

They began performing a necessary operation - an amputation, a disembowelling, a leeching of all the theatrical rottenness that was still buried within me.

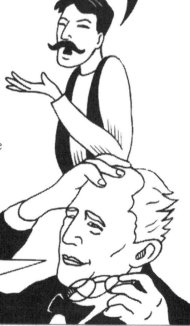

It was a painful operation for Stanislavski.

Something in me gave way. All that was old was useless, and there was nothing new.

In rehearsal, Fedotov showed him how to play the role.
But there's a big difference between seeing something done, and doing it yourself.

"Live it through, feel it stronger, deeper, live it!" they say. Or, "You are not living it through! You must live it through! Try to feel it!" And you try, and exert all your strength, and tie yourself in knots, and squeeze your voice until it is hoarse, your eyes pop out of their sockets, and the blood rushes to your head till you feel giddy.

At one point, in an attempt to find the true feeling for the role, Stanislavski went to a medieval castle and asked to be locked in a cellar overnight.

It was terrifying and lonely, dark, there were rats, it was damp - and all these inconveniences stopped me concentrating on the role. And when in the darkness I began to repeat the text that had become so hateful to me - it all just seemed so stupid.

He hammered on the door. But as he had told the caretaker not to let him out on any account, the door stayed locked.

The only result was a bad cold.

Something else, it seems, was necessary...

But what? It seemed one had to raise oneself to a higher plane. But how to get there - no one would tell me.

HIGH PAVEMENT
COLLE

17

On the same bill with *The Miserly Knight*, he played Sotanville in Molière's *Georges Dandin*.

There were fixed ways of playing Molière. On holiday in Paris, Stanislavski had seen the Comédie-Française, and loved all the theatrical hokum - the plumed hats, the courtly bows and flourishes - that constituted the Molière "style." In rehearsal, he began copying everything he'd seen, and felt "completely at home." Once again, Fedotov just laughed. And again, Stanislavski realised that he had to abandon the "*old*," the conventional tricks of the stage, and look for something new. He could not simply copy somebody else's performance - however good. He had to create something *himself*. Stanislavski knew he had to *live* the role, not simply *play* at living it.

The hardest thing of all is to stand on the boards, and really believe and take seriously everything that happens on the stage. But without belief and seriousness, it is impossible to play comedy or satire... especially Molière.

He found the "life" in the part by accident. Something in his make-up gave a living and comic expression to his face. It was a moment of great joy. He began to live the role, rather than copy somebody else.

Something, somewhere, turned within me. All that was dim became clear; all that was groundless suddenly had ground under it; and everything I didn't believe in - now I could believe it.

In his notes after the performance, Stanislavski observed a curious paradox about acting.

It's strange : when you feel right - the impression on the audience is worse; when you control yourself and don't surrender completely to the role - it is better.

In the past, when he felt "inspired" on stage, he had lost all self-control. Now he realised it is not possible to act like that.

I had mistaken simple stage emotion, which is a kind of hysteria, for real inspiration.

For the next play, *A Bitter Fate* by Pisemski, Stanislavski set himself a new problem: to achieve greater self-control and restraint. He tried to eliminate every unnecessary gesture and movement. He taught himself to stand motionless like a wooden Indian. However, he achieved this only at cost of great physical strain, so he tried to focus all the strain in one area - digging his fingernails into the palms of his hand, for example, until he drew blood...

This seemed to free the rest of his body, even if only temporarily. At times, he felt he achieved something of the *relaxation* on stage he so admired in actors like Salvini. The audience was amazed at the calm and truthfulness of his acting.

He tried not only to cut out movement, but also to *hide* his feelings. He found that the more he tried to appear calm, the more the emotion boiled inside him. Then, in the play's climactic mob scene, he gave himself up, against his will, to the atmosphere of excitement. He could no longer control his gestures and feared he would be reprimanded for loss of control. Instead, he was praised for showing the emotion simmering inside him, until it could be held in no longer. He had shown a development from *piano* to *forte*.

It was an important technical lesson, demonstrating the need for a sense of *progression* - building by degrees to the climax of a role.

STANISLAVSKI PRACTICES STANDING STILL LIKE A WOODEN INDIAN

CIGARS

Working with Fedotov had changed Stanislavski's acting forever. He was now determined to wage war against the clichés and routine "lies" of the stage. He declared:

I began to hate the "theatre" in the theatre...

The professional Russian theatre at the time was in a poor state. It was dominated by the star system; there was little sense of an "ensemble." Plays were staged with only a few rehearsals. Directors didn't really exist; a stage manager gave the moves. Design was virtually non-existent. Furniture and settings, costumes and props, were simply taken from stock - with no concern for period style or historical accuracy.

There were talented actors; but there was also plenty of bad acting, based on tired theatrical traditions. There were set ways of expressing different emotions -

...showing your teeth and rolling the whites of your eyes when you are jealous

...tearing your hair to show despair

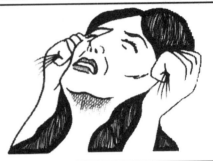

- and fixed ways of playing certain roles (Stanislavski called them "stencils")

...peasants always spat on the floor

...and aristocrats played with their lorgnettes

There was no "life" in these traditions, no "truth." Stanislavski declared:

These are the very forms that we must ruthlessly drive out of the theatre, using every means at our disposal.

When he directed Pisemski's play, *Burning Letters* in 1889, he told the actors to avoid false, theatrical gestures. He wanted a sense of them *"living through"* their roles - even in the pauses. Everything should be *"simple, natural, elegant, and, above all, artistic."*

We introduced a new manner of acting, never before seen on the Russian stage... The intelligent, sensitive public sensed this and went wild with delight; the traditionalists protested.

In the final play of the Society's first season, however - Schiller's *Kabale und Liebe* - Stanislavski went back to some of his bad old ways. He played the role of Ferdinand, dressed in long boots and with a sword. But there was a difference. He acted opposite Maria Perevoshchikova (stage name - Lilina). They were in love and didn't know it - but it showed in their acting. They kissed each other just a little too naturally. On July 5 1889, they were married.

In its first year, the Society ran up a large deficit, and it was forced to limit its activities. The Hunting Club took over the Society's premises. Fedotov and Komissarzhevski both left; but Stanislavski soldiered on.

In the first production of the new season, A Law Unto Themselves by Ostrovski, he played the role of Imshin. He used technical means to create the movement of an old man. Again, he was working from the "outer to the inner, from the body to the soul."

But it was a rather one-note performance. One day, he was watching rehearsals for another play. From the auditorium, Stanislavski could see the mistakes the actors were making, and offered them some advice...

When you play a whiner, look for where is happy and robust... When you play a good man, look for where he is evil, and in an evil man look for where he is good.

Suddenly, he realised his own mistake with Imshin:

I played a beast... but there was no need to take care of that, the author himself had taken care of it, and it was left to me to find where he is good, suffering, remorseful, loving, tender, unselfish...

It was an important discovery, creating greater depth and complexity in his acting.

The agreement with the Hunting Club meant that the Society had to present a new play every week. This was a great strain. They were helped by professional directors who showed them how to achieve quick results, using all the old conventional methods of acting. They had the illusion of great and productive work. But later Stanislavski saw it did not help his artistic development, but harmed it. Then, in Lent 1890, the Meiningen Court Theatre performed in Moscow. The company - led by **Georg II**, the Duke of Saxe-Meiningen (in Germany) - were the theatrical sensation of the day. All the elements of production - the **mises en scène**, the scenery, the lighting and sound effects - were carefully prepared and co-ordinated to create an artistic whole. Settings were designed to suggest a real environment, rather than a theatrical "set." They were based on meticulous historical research. For Maria Stuart the designers reproduced the Palace of Westminster. For *Julius Caesar* they reconstructed the Roman forum. Real swords, goblets and helmets were preferred to stage props.

GEORG II, DUKE OF SAXE-MEININGEN

The company's aim was not simply archaeological reconstruction. The sets were designed as dynamic and three-dimensional acting spaces. The use of different levels, platforms and steps helped to keep the action moving fluidly and create interesting stage pictures.

The acting was not very distinguished - but the crowd scenes were stunning. These were not crowds of spear-carriers, standing stiffly in the background. They filled the stage with a continuous pattern of movement. In *Julius Caesar*, the citizens of Rome reacted so wildly when Mark Antony read Caesar's will, audiences felt as if a revolution was really about to break out.

See that? Now that's the kind of acting I'm looking for.

Stanislavski did not miss a single performance. The director's striking stage compositions impressed him, and the way lighting and sound effects were used to create a powerful mood, capturing the "essence" of a scene.

He tried to find out everything he could about the Meininger's working methods. The company largely rejected the "star system" and aimed instead for a sense of an "ensemble." All power was in the hands of the stage-director, Ludwig Chronegk. He enforced strict discipline on the actors. At the start of rehearsals, he would ring a large bell, and order work to begin in a quiet but intimidating voice...

"Anfangen..."

It seemed to Stanislavski that there were parallels between the Meiningen Theatre and the Society of Art and Literature:

We also wanted to create large-scale productions, to reveal profound thoughts and feelings, but, because we did not have enough competent actors, we had to give all the power to the director.

Besides...

I liked Chronegk's self-control and cold-bloodedness. I imitated him...

LUDWIG CHRONEGK

27

For a time, Stanislavski became a despotic director. The new regime began with his next production - Tolstoy's *The Fruits of the Enlightenment* (1891). Like Chronegk, he acquired a bell to signal the start of rehearsals. He controlled all elements of the production, planned all the moves in advance, and drilled his cast until they got it right.

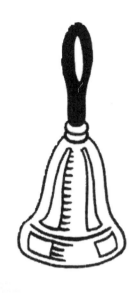

I showed the actors what I saw in my imagination, and they copied me.

The influence of the Meiningen Theatre was seen in other ways. Stanislavski's preparations for plays now usually began with meticulous historical research. For his production of *Foma* (an adaptation of a story by Dostoevsky), he produced preliminary sketches for designers, and insisted the sets and costumes should reflect the period (the 1850s). Sound and lighting effects were used to create a powerful "mood."

Stanislavski played Rostanev. He seemed to find the character intuitively - without the usual tortures of creation. He *believed* everything in the role. He did not copy someone else's performance; he *became* Rostanev:

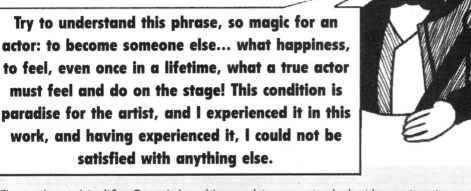

Try to understand this phrase, so magic for an actor: to become someone else... what happiness, to feel, even once in a lifetime, what a true actor must feel and do on the stage! This condition is paradise for the artist, and I experienced it in this work, and having experienced it, I could not be satisfied with anything else.

*Throughout his life, Stanislavski sought ways to help the actor to achieve this "condition" : to find the "secret sources of inspiration"; **to become someone else.***

For his production of *Uriel Acosta* by Gutskov (1895), Stanislavski created a stunning visual spectacle, through the sets and costumes. The crowd scenes were highly choreographed. In one scene, when an angry mob rushed towards the footlights, spectators in the front row of the stalls jumped in fear.

The production became the talk of Moscow. But Stanislavski was not entirely satisfied with his own performance. He felt unable to reach the emotional climaxes in the role of the hero. The more you try to force an emotion, he saw, the more it resists and throws out invisible spiritual buffers. It is like being asked to leap across a wide chasm. You resist, because you feel your own helplessness, and the impossibility of making that leap.

In 1896, he staged *Othello*.

He had dreamed of playing the role, ever since he saw Salvini's great performance. Now, he found a "model" for Othello in real life. On vacation in Paris, he met an Arab in a restaurant, and dined with him. Later, in his hotel, Stanislavski stood for half the night before a mirror, putting on sheets and towels, trying to turn himself into the Moor of Venice.

He still felt he could not achieve the heights of passion. He was straining so hard that it made him ill. After rehearsal he had to lie down, his heart thumping, his throat sore...

This isn't art! Salvini is old enough to be my father, but he isn't exhausted after a performance.

The famous Italian actor, **Ernesto Rossi**, saw the play, and asked Stanislavski to come and see him.

God gave you everything for the stage, for Othello, for the whole Shakespearean repertoire. It's in your own hands. All you need is art. It will come, of course –

But where can I learn that art? How ? From whom?

Mm-a! If there is no great artist near you whom you can trust, I can recommend only one teacher.

Who is it? Who?

You yourself.

The production was based on careful research. Stanislavski went to Venice and brought back sketches and props. The results were reflected in the sets and costumes.

This kind of exhaustive historical authenticity has been dubbed "*Meiningenitis*." However, Stanislavski was not interested in naturalism for its own sake.

The chief merit of his work at that time, he believed, lay in his "*search for the truth*" and his rejection of "lies, especially theatrical, mechanical lies."

I sought living, real life in the theatre - not ordinary life, of course, but artistic life.

An externally truthful *mise en scène* could help to eliminate theatrical falsehood.

This is Stanislavski's description of the opening of *Othello* :

The play began with the far-off striking of a tower clock. These sounds, so banal now, made an impression in their time. There was a distant splash of oars (we invented this sound as well); a floating gondola came to a stop on the stage, there was a thunder of chains as it was tied to a painted Venetian pile; then the gondola gently swayed in the water.

The sound effects created a strong and dramatic atmosphere or mood for the scene.

Stanislavski gave the actors precise instructions. The actor playing Iago, for example, was told to dip his hands into the water of the canal (and the water was *real* - it was in a hidden washtub next to the gondola). This concentration on realistic details of behaviour helped the actors to avoid theatrical clichés, and to find a sense of *truth or belief* in their roles.

The truth awoke emotion, and emotion stirred the artistic intuition.
It was another way of going from the external to the internal.

Other productions in this period show Stanislavski's interest in **non-realistic** drama - and his love of dramatic scenic effects.

We hate the theatrical in the theatre, but we love the scenic on the stage. That is an enormous difference.

In **Gerhart Hauptmann's** *The Assumption of Hannele* (1896), which he staged with professional actors, he achieved a stunning climactic scene. In a bluish light, the characters moved like figures in a nightmare, and the stage was filled with mysterious sounds, and penetrating cries and whispers.

Part of Stanislavski was still a showman. He confessed :

I like to create mischief in the theatre. I'm happy when I succeed in finding a trick which deceives the audience.

The Polish Jew (1896) contained a dream sequence so frightening that some people in the audience fainted.

In 1898 Stanislavski staged Hauptmann's *The Sunken Bell*. The play has a fantastic fairy-tale plot. For the first time, he worked with the designer, **Viktor Simov**.

Together they created a three-dimensional set, with hills, hollows and trees. The actors could not walk on the set at all. It was what Stanislavski wanted.

Let them climb or sit on stones, leap on the rocks, balance or crawl along the branches of the trees.

This again forced the actors to abandon theatrical clichés, and play in a way that was "*new to the stage.*" Their movements had to be plastic and expressive.

A noted critic and playwright called **Vladimir Nemirovich-Danchenko** saw the production and wrote: "The *mise en scène* astonished you by its wealth of imagination, innovation and invention." He was particularly impressed by the use of pauses, and the atmospheric sound effects - "the inhuman cries and voices, the whistling of nocturnal birds" - which were like a musical score to accompany the play.

It was the last production of the Society of Art and Literature. In nine years, Stanislavski had turned it into the most innovative theatre group in Moscow. But he had been thinking for some time about creating a professional company. In June, 1897, while on holiday, he had received a message from Nemirovich-Danchenko, scribbled on the back of a visiting card:

I am told you are expected back in Moscow tomorrow, on Wednesday. I shall be at the Slav Bazaar at one o'clock. Could we meet there?

В.. Куур..

They met at the Slavyanski Bazaar, a restaurant in the centre of Moscow, on 22 June 1897. Over lunch, they talked...

And talked...   And talked...

Both deplored the current state of the professional Russian theatre. They agreed to form a new kind of company, dedicated to establishing theatre once more as a serious art form ; a revolutionary theatre, with a revolutionary programme:

We rebelled against the old manner of acting, against theatricality, against false pathos, declamation and artificiality, against bad conventions of staging and decor... against the whole system of production, and the contemptible repertoire, in theatres at that time.

As well as being a playwright, Nemirovich taught acting at the Philharmonic School. The core of the new company, they agreed, would be formed from the Society of Art and Literature, and Nemirovich's students. They wanted to create better conditions for actors to work in. At the same time, they would demand high standards of "artistic ethics" They set down their ideals in a series of aphorisms:

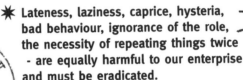

✳ **There are no small roles, only small actors.**

✳ **Today - Hamlet, tomorrow - an extra, but even as an extra, you must be an artist.**

✳ **The playwright, the actor, the artist, the dresser, the stage-hand - all serve one goal: the idea, which is at the heart of the play.**

✳ **Every violation of the creative life of the theatre is a crime.**

✳ **Lateness, laziness, caprice, hysteria, bad behaviour, ignorance of the role, the necessity of repeating things twice - are equally harmful to our enterprise and must be eradicated.**

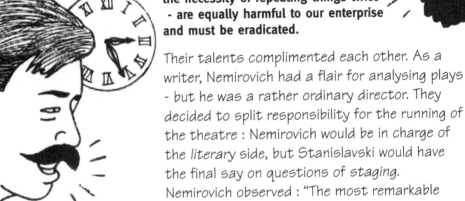

Their talents complimented each other. As a writer, Nemirovich had a flair for analysing plays - but he was a rather ordinary director. They decided to split responsibility for the running of the theatre : Nemirovich would be in charge of the *literary* side, but Stanislavski would have the final say on questions of *staging*.
Nemirovich observed : "The most remarkable thing about this conversation was that we never once argued."
They could not foresee that in later years, they would argue about almost everything...

They finally stopped talking, 18 hours later, over breakfast at Stanislavski's home. Nemirovich recalled they were "like men possessed":

We have no doubt that we have the strength and we can do it. We can do everything. We know everything; we know what has to be done, and how to do it.

The new company took over a year to set up. The main problem facing them was simple :

Money, money, and money.

Nemirovich assumed Stanislavski would finance the company from his own private wealth. However, after his experience with the Society, Stanislavski insisted on a public company, financed by shareholders. Attempts to raise the money at first met with a brick wall, until Savva Morozov, a railway magnate, stepped in.

He put up a lot of the money to launch the company and continued to support it for several years.

And so, the means have been found. We will have a theatre.

I just hope he doesn't try to interfere in the company's artistic work.

HIGH PAVEMENT

On June 14, 1898, the company assembled for the first time. They had been given the use of a barn to rehearse in, on an estate in the village of Pushkino, some fifty miles from Moscow. The company lived and worked together like a commune. Everyone took turns to clean the rehearsal space. Stanislavski was first on the duty rota. He was not very experienced in domestic matters. On the first day, he lit the samovar - but forgot to put any water in.

The samovar melted ...

He began rehearsals with discussions of the play, and then rehearsed slowly, working on a scene for hours, even days. This was quite new for most of the actors. (The usual practice in other theatres was to run whole Acts at once). For every play, he prepared a detailed production plan in advance, setting down every move and every gesture, as well as describing the scenery, costumes, make-up, and so on.

It was a way of working that Stanislavski later strongly rejected. But in these early days of the Art Theatre, the method ensured every production expressed a coherent vision.

For the first season, the company rented a small theatre called the Ermitazh (or "Hermitage"), some distance from the city centre. When Stanislavski went there for the first time, he was very excited. Here, at last, was his own theatre space.

In this theatre we can build the life we have dreamt about for so long; we can cleanse art of all pollution, and create a temple instead of a fairground side-show.

The building was in a terrible state. With no money, they had to try to make it bearable and turn it into "a temple."

Stanislavski and Nemirovich still had not settled on a title for the theatre. They wanted it to be **"popular"** and **"accessible,"** appealing to a different kind of audience - students, professionals, the middle and lower classes. Various titles were considered: The Popular Theatre, The Dramatic Theatre, The Moscow Theatre... Finally, in the middle of a rehearsal, Nemirovich suddenly interrupted Stanislavski.

It is impossible to wait any longer. I propose to call our theatre "The Moscow Art and Popular Theatre" ...Do you agree? - Yes or no?

Taken unawares, Stanislavski said :

Yes

In its third season, the theatre had to drop the term Popular from the title, because it had to increase ticket prices in order to make ends meet.

It became simply **The Moscow Art Theatre**.

The new theatre opened on 14 October 1898, with a production of *Tsar Fyodor Ioannovich* by **Aleksei Tolstoy**, a drama about medieval Russia. Stanislavski chose it because he thought it would be a crowd-pleaser; it contained plenty of opportunities for spectacle. To some extent, he felt a lavish production, and an audacious mise-en-scène, were necessary to disguise the shortcomings and inexperience of the actors. But he was also determined not to present the conventional, clichéd view of Russia which could be seen in other theatres; he wanted to create a *new* way of performing historical drama, which would oust the old forever.

IVAN MOSKVIN AS TSAR FYODOR

Again, he undertook extensive research. But he was interested, less in strict historical accuracy, than in creating the atmosphere of another time and another world. He looked for what would work **"scenically."**

Simov's designs were stunning. The most striking was the set for the garden in Act Three. The audience watched the action through a line of birch trees, which stretched *right across the footlights*. To the actors, this seemed like "a complete revolution, delighting them by its truth and boldness." It was like a fourth wall between the audience and stage. But it did not exclude the audience - it made them feel almost as if they were in the garden themselves, eavesdropping on events...

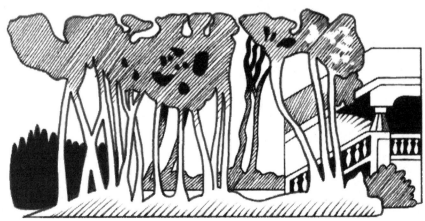

Again, there were spectacular crowd scenes. Stanislavski provided detailed character biographies for the actors in these scenes, so that, even if they did not have a single line to say, they could still create *living* characters.

On the first night, Stanislavski was very nervous. On stage, he tried give the actors a last minute pep talk. In the middle of it, the orchestra on the other side of the curtain started to play the overture.

There was nothing left for me to do but to begin to dance, in order to give vent to the energy boiling inside me, which I wanted to convey to my young comrades-in-arms. I danced, singing and shouting out encouraging phrases, with a white, deathly face, with frightened eyes, with broken breath and convulsive gestures. This, my tragic dance, was later dubbed "The Dance of Death."

The actors were nonplussed. A stage assistant intervened.

Konstantin Sergeyevich, leave the stage! At once! Don't upset the actors!

Sheepishly, Stanislavski went away and locked himself in his dressing room...

The production was a success but the critics in the press were grudging:

It was as if they said, "Let's wait and see what will happen next..."

Some people complained that the sets and costumes overwhelmed the actor; others argued :

"It's an imitation of the Meiningen Theatre, and nothing more!"

It took a long time for Stanislavski to shake off the reputation of copying the Meiningen Theatre.

The productions that followed - including *The Sunken Bell* and *The Merchant of Venice* - made very little impact. Ticket sales were not good enough to cover costs. It began to look as if the theatre might have to close. Everything depended on the success of a play by **Anton Chekhov**, *The Seagull*, which opened on December 17.

The *Seagull* was unlike anything Stanislavski had staged before. Chekhov himself described the play as a comedy with "lots of talk about literature, little action, tons of love." It had been staged first at the Aleksandrinski Theatre in St. Petersburg in 1896, where it failed dismally. Critics said it didn't seem like a play at all, with its apparent lack of external action and conflict.

Part of the problem was that the Aleksandrinksi production was staged in the conventional way, with few rehearsals, and scenery taken from stock. Chekhov complained that the actors were "acting too much"; it was too "theatrical." It seemed that the old methods of acting and staging could not cope with Chekhov's work.

We were fortunate to find a new approach to Chekhov.

But at first, Stanislavski thought the play monotonous, and unsuitable for the stage. Nemirovich spent many hours trying to explain it to him - stressing the play's lyrical qualities, and the "atmosphere, the aroma and mood, which envelop the characters." Still not entirely convinced, Stanislavski went away to write the production plan...

The production of *The Seagull* has sometimes been seen as the acme of stage naturalism. But it was in fact a highly *poetic* rendering of the play. Stanislavski used lighting, sound, and setting, to soak the play in an overwhelming atmosphere. Here, for example, are his notes for the opening of Act 1:

> *The play begins in darkness. An evening in August. The dim light of a lantern, the distant singing of a drunkard out on a spree, the distant howling of a dog, the croaking of frogs, the cry of a corncrake, and the occasional tolling of a distant church-bell - help the audience to feel the sad, monotonous life of the characters.*

The production was daring in its devices. Across the forestage, near the footlights, Stanislavski and Simov placed a long bench (creating a kind of "fourth wall" between stage and audience). In one scene, the actors sat on a bench with their backs to the audience. A significant innovation consisted in the use of **pauses**, which made the dialogue seem "nearer to life" - but they also helped create the mood of the performance.

On the first night, the actors were extremely nervous.

How would the audience respond to the play?

Would they be able to appreciate it?

Moreover, the actors had heard that Chekhov was ill with tuberculosis. They feared if the play failed again, as it had in Petersburg, it might kill him... No wonder, then, that many of them took valerian drops (a form of tranquilliser) before the performance began.

At the end of Act One, the curtain was drawn. Then, silence. Nobody clapped. The actors decided that the play had failed. But suddenly...

It was as if a dam had broken, or a bomb exploded - all at once there was a deafening burst of applause.

The audience was spellbound throughout by the powerful, compelling mood of the performance. At the end, Nemirovich sent a telegram to Chekhov:

ANTON CHEKHOV

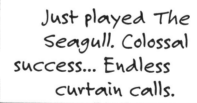

Just played The Seagull. Colossal success... Endless curtain calls.

With this triumph, Nemirovich declared :

The New Theatre was born.

When Stanislavski staged *The Seagull*, he had not even begun to develop his "system" of acting. Nevertheless, he saw Chekhov's work as an important influence on his thinking, helping to pave the way for the "system." He declared:

In Chekhov's plays it is wrong to try to act, to perform. You must be - that is, you must live, exist, following the deep, inner, spiritual line of development.

Stanislavski called this,

the line of intuition and feeling.

The appeal of Chekhov's work, he argued, does not lie in the dialogue. The actor has to create the *inner life* of the character that lies concealed beneath the dialogue, in the "sub-text."

Staging *The Seagull*, he discovered ways to help the actors to find this inner life, and to "live" on stage. In his production notebooks, Stanislavski set down a whole range of activities for the characters. So for example in Act I, someone "unhurriedly takes out a small comb and during the whole of the next scene (sitting with his back to the audience) he combs his beard, then takes off his hat, combs his hair, straightens and does up his ti

This helped to create a sense of continuous "life" on the stage. The actors carried on with their actions, even as another actor was speaking.

Performing the actions also helped the actors' concentration. It was as if they were acting with an imaginary fourth wall between the stage and the auditorium.

The powerful "mood" of the production influenced the actors, touching unconscious emotional chords:

They felt external truth, and intimate memories of their own lives arose in their souls, enticing from them the feelings which Chekhov was talking about. In such moments the actor stopped playing, and began to live the role, became the character... It was a creative miracle.

After seeing the production, a friend wrote to Chekhov: "the performers do not act a play called The Seagull, but life itself."

"The new methods of Chekhov's drama," Stanislavski said, "served as the basis for our future artistic development." The company continued to explore "the line of intuition and feeling," in a whole series of productions.

МОСКОВСКІЙ ХУДОЖЕСТВЕННЬІЙ ТЕАТРЪ

MOSCOW ART THEATRE LOGO

In future years, the Art Theatre became known as the **House of Chekhov**, and a seagull was chosen as the theatre's emblem. *Uncle Vanya* was staged in 1899, and then Chekhov wrote *Three Sisters* (1901) and *The Cherry Orchard* (1904) especially for the company. He even married the actress, Olga Knipper. It has to be said that he had very mixed feelings about Stanislavski's productions and felt there was an over-reliance on sound effects. Once he famously joked:

> Listen, I will write a new play, and it will begin like this: "How wonderful, how quiet! No birds, no dogs, no cuckoos... not one single cricket can be heard."

More seriously, he argued that Stanislavski made the plays too heavy, missing the element of comedy. After the premiere of *The Cherry Orchard*, he declared:

OLGA KNIPPER

> It's all wrong, the play and the performance. That isn't what I saw, they couldn't understand what I wanted.

In later years, Nemirovich reflected:

> Our theatre was at fault - there's no denying it - in simply failing to understand Chekhov... it was a long time before we succeeded in capturing the subtle texture of his work; perhaps the theatre handled him too roughly...

In 1900, Stanislavski played Doctor Stockman in a version of Henrik Ibsen's *An Enemy of the People* (1900). Stockman is an idealist, who is determined to fight for the truth - however unpopular this makes him. Some saw parallels between Stockman, and Stanislavski himself, fighting against all forms of lies in the theatre. Certainly, he seemed to identify with the role.

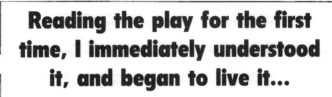

Reading the play for the first time, I immediately understood it, and began to live it...

He discovered the character's *"through line of action"* in the play, the idea or goal that drives him:
Stockman's love for *truth*.

Intuitively, he found the *"inner image"* of the role - Stockman's youthful movements, his happiness, his love of jokes...

And then he found the *outer image* of the role, its physical form. *This was a* **significant turning point.**

In the past, Stanislavski had tended to work from the **external** *to the* **internal**. *However, in creating Stockman, he began with the* **internal** *- and the* **external** *seemed to follow naturally, intuitively.*

He made Stockman a thin, stooping figure, with two fingers of his hand stretched out, as if to prod his listeners, and hammer his points home.

And so, by degrees, "the soul and body of Stockman and Stanislavski became one organically." Again he felt the greatest joy an artist can feel - *to become another.* The transformation was complete. Other actors who came near him on stage were convinced that they were in the presence of a different person.

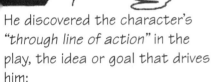

On 13 March, 1901, the production was performed at a theatre in St. Petersburg. Earlier that day, a student demonstration in Kazanski Square had been brutally broken up by the authorities ; several students were killed, and many were arrested. In the evening, when they were released, some of them went to the Art Theatre...

In the last Act of the play, Stockman returns home from a hostile meeting, where he has been physically jostled. He looks at the tears in his clothes, and says :

When you go to fight for freedom and truth, you shouldn't put on a new pair of trousers.

The line sent an electric charge through the audience, which was already highly excited. The applause turned into a stormy demonstration. People even jumped on to the stage in order to embrace Doctor Stockman. The production, and Stanislavski's performance, had become a major political event.

But Stanislavski was not trying to make a political statement in the play. He had concentrated simply on creating the character, and *living the role*, along the **"line of intuition and feeling."** Paradoxically, this seemed to increase the play's impact. In *"political"* plays, Stanislavski believed, the actor should not try to think too much about the *"message,"* but should **"live with the thoughts and feelings of the role."** The *"message"* would then emerge naturally, by itself.

While Stanislavski maintained that theatre should reflect the concerns of the age, he did not believe it should become a simple platform for propaganda. However, in the period leading up to the **First Revolution in 1905**, the Art Theatre in many ways became a focus for liberal opposition to the Tsarist regime. Audiences came to see plays, which reflected the general mood of discontent. **Maksim Gorky**, already a popular rebel and a former political prisoner, wrote especially for the theatre.

In October 1902, the Art Theatre moved to its new home, on Kamergerski Lane, in centre of Moscow. Morozov largely paid for the move. The first production was Gorky's *Philistines* - followed, in December, by his most famous play, *The Lower Depths*, in which he confronted Moscow audiences with a world they had never seen before: the life of the homeless, in society's *"lower depths."*

GORKY

To prepare for the production, the company made a visit to Khitrov Market, where many of Moscow's homeless lived.

We freely looked around the large dormitories with countless plank beds, where many tired people were lying, men and women, looking like corpses.

The excursion inspired Stanislavski's imagination. He wanted to make audiences feel anger at the senseless sufferings of these outcasts. Moreover, he felt he now understood the "inner meaning" of the play.

> **"Freedom - whatever the cost!" That's at the heart of the play. The freedom for which people sink to the lower depths of life, unaware that there, they become slaves.**

The production was a great success. Olga Knipper said:

> It was almost like the first performance of "The Seagull." A similar triumph... The audience went wild... Our theatre has been born again.

In the space of just a few years, the Art Theatre had become a Mecca for Moscow's theatregoers. Other theatres throughout Russia began to copy its productions. But now, it came under attack. The symbolist poet, Valeri Bryusov, wrote an article called *Unnecessary Truth*, in which he accused the Art Theatre of propagating a form of crude naturalism.

VALERI BRYUSOV

> Contemporary theatres seek to reproduce life as truthfully as possible. They think they are suitably fulfilling their purpose if everything on stage is just as it is in life. The actors try to speak as they do in drawing rooms, the set designers copy scenes from nature, the costume designers cut their costumes in line with archaeological data.

Bryusov called for a stylised theatre and declared:

> **"It is time for the theatre to stop imitating reality."**

Stanislavski maintained that the Art Theatre had *never* sought naturalism on the stage. The aim was always what he called **spiritual realism** : an *inner* rather than an *outer* **"truth"**; the truth of the actor's feelings and experience.

Unfortunately, Bryusov's article in many ways set the terms of the debate for years to come. He had labelled the Art Theatre *"naturalistic"* and the label stuck. In later years, Stanislavski observed:

> **This misunderstanding has taken root and still exists today, despite the fact that in the last quarter of a century we have passed through the most varied and even conflicting stages of artistic development and have experienced a whole series of changes and renewals.**

Stanislavski recognised that, in the early years, some of the theatre's productions veered towards *naturalism*. When he staged **Leo Tolstoy's** *The Power of Darkness* (1902), for example, he said he wanted to follow "the line of intuition and feeling," but "against my will, something went wrong and I unexpectedly found myself producing the play on the line of ordinary, everyday life" - *naturalistically*. There was no *inner life* to the performances.

Stanislavski was also unhappy about a production of *Julius Caesar* (1903), staged by Nemirovich in the *Meiningen* style.

Endless research went into preparing the sets and costumes; the results were so accurate that parties of school children came to the production just to learn about life in Ancient Rome. The acting was overwhelmed by all the naturalistic detail.

"POWER OF DARKNESS" (TOLSTOY)

Stanislavski was persuaded to shave off his moustache in order to play Brutus.

BEFORE

AFTER

During rehearsals, Stanislavski hoped the actors would learn to live as naturally in a Shakespeare play as in one by Chekhov. Nevertheless, his own performance refused to come to life - perhaps because Nemirovich imposed **his** interpretation of Brutus on him. The production may have helped to convince Stanislavski that an actor cannot be **made** to feel, on the orders of the director.

The Art Theatre, Stanislavski believed, had run into a "blind alley"; as an actor, he was stagnating. Looking for new directions, he became interested in the fashionable **symbolist** movement. Plays by writers such as the Belgian dramatist **Maurice Maeterlinck** were far removed from naturalism. They were full of **"sublime feelings"** and **"a sense of the mysteries of existence."** They seemed to demand new forms of acting.

We had already learnt to live on the stage by the things that stirred us in life. What we lacked was something else: I mean those artistic means that help actors to live through great abstract feelings.

Stanislavski began working alone again, in the silence of the night. He hunted for new ways of moving and speaking, which went beyond realism, but found that all the old, bad, theatrical ways returned. Yet, there were moments when he felt inspired.

Where does that come from? It is a secret of nature!

VSEVOLOD MEYERHOLD

It seemed that when he *felt* something emotionally, then his voice and body responded. He began to find the "simplicity and nobility" he was looking for. So he tried to *make* himself feel the emotion, to become "inspired." But the results were only physical tension and strain.

In his despair, Stanislavski found the man he thought could help him. Vsevolod Meyerhold...

Meyerhold had been a founder member of the Art Theatre; he played Treplev in *The Seagull*. In 1902, he had left, to form his own company in the provinces, where he experimented with new forms, including symbolist drama. Now the men met again.

The difference between us was that I only strained towards the new, without knowing how to achieve it, whereas Meyerhold, it seemed, had already found new ways and methods.

Together, they planned to open a *Theatre-Studio* and hoped it would initiate a revolution in the theatre. It was based on a **"symbolist"** programme. Stanislavski declared:

The time for the unreal has arrived on the stage. It is necessary to portray life, not as it flows in reality, but as we vaguely sense it in dreams, in visions, in moments of sublime inspiration.

Officially, the new venture was an offshoot of the Art Theatre, but it was heavily subsidised by Stanislavski himself.

Like the Art Theatre in its first season, the new company met to rehearse during the summer, in a barn near Pushkino. At first, the work seemed to be going well; then came the first dress rehearsal of Maeterlinck's *Death of Tintagiles*.

Meyerhold had tried to create a stylised form of movement: slow, deliberate, almost ritualistic. At significant moments the actors froze, like living statues.

At first, the stage was in semi-darkness. Only the silhouettes of the actors were visible. Suddenly Stanislavski, sitting in the auditorium, cried out,

Lights!

It was too dark, he insisted; an audience won't stand darkness for long on stage.

You need to see the actors' faces!

The lights were raised and made the failings of the production all too apparent. The actors were unable to cope with the stylised movement. There was no inner life.

Meyerhold had tried to cover the acting weaknesses with his staging. The result was that the actors were "simply clay in his hands for the modelling of beautiful groupings and mises en scène."

Stanislavski was no longer interested in "the external means of production and the tricks of the director." He was now convinced "that the theatre above all else is for the actor and cannot exist without him, that the new drama needs new actors, with a completely new technique."

All my hopes were pinned on the actor and the development of a firm basis for his creativity and technique.

Meyerhold later saw that, even then, "elements of an early version of his 'system' were forming in Stanislavski's mind."

The opening of the new theatre was postponed. Then, in October 1905, Russia saw a wave of strikes and demonstrations, and mutinies in both the army and navy - the so-called First Revolution. In Moscow, there was fighting on the streets, and for a time all theatre performances were prohibited. Stanislavski decided to close the Studio for good - at a personal loss of some 80,000 roubles. He spent years trying to repay the debt.

The Studio experiment had failed, and yet...

...for all that, our theatre found its future among the ruins.

Act IV: First Thoughts on the "System"

The tense political situation in Russia continued throughout the autumn. Stanislavski and Nemirovich decided to take the company on its first tour abroad, to cities in Europe. It was a great success; but one night on stage, Stanislavski suddenly felt his whole performance was mechanical and dead. He was making the same gestures and moves he always did, but there was no real emotion, no life inside.
He lost all faith in himself as an actor.

In the summer, he went to Finland for a holiday. Every morning, he sat on a cliff overlooking the sea, taking stock of his life.

When he began work on a role, he was filled by a sense of "a beautiful, exciting, inner truth." As time went by, and he played the role over and over again, the "feeling of truth" was lost. Salvini had declared:

> Every great actor must feel, and especially he should feel the thing he is portraying. I even find he must feel this emotion not only once or twice, while he is studying his role, but to a greater or lesser degree at every performance, whether it is the first, or the thousandth ...

But Stanislavs[ki]
did not know ho[w]
to achieve th[is]

How can roles be saved from degeneration, from spiritual decay?

64

He returned to Moscow, his problems still unsolved. Suddenly he saw that the actor's position on stage is completely unnatural. It is very difficult to feel real emotion when you are standing in front of a crowd of strangers, with their eyes fixed upon you, waiting for you to move them, to make them laugh and cry. You might have to play a love scene, but you don't feel like a great "lover." Instead, you just feel very self-conscious and embarrassed. You know that the audience must hear your every word, and so you yell the words of love which, in real life, you would only whisper. And you have to make your gestures large enough to be seen by the people in the cheap seats at the back.

an you really think about love, let alone feel the sensation of love, in such circumstances? All you can do is strive and strain and over-exert yourself, from a sense of your own impotence, and the impossibility of the task.

Small wonder, then, that the actor often resorts to empty clichés, to represent unfelt emotions. And this, Stanislavski concluded, is the actor's normal state. There is a painful and debilitating split between the internal and the external, between body and soul. Having recognised this, he began to seek a different physical and spiritual state on stage, which would help, and not stifle, the actor's creativity.

He called this "the creative state"...

What is the "creative state"? Stanislavski himself is rather vague. He says that the actor who is in a creative state on stage feels,

"I'm in good spirits today! I'm at my best!"

"I'm acting with pleasure!"

Most significantly, perhaps, the actor feels,

"Today I am living my role."

It is, then, the kind of state he had experienced himself, when playing Rostanev in *Foma*, or when he first played Dr. Stockman. When you are carried away by the play, and live the role, you "suddenly, unexpectedly rise to great artistic heights, and thrill the audience. In such moments the artist lives or creates by inspiration."

Great actors, Stanislavski saw, seem able to find the "creative state" every time they play a role. For most actors, it happens only intermittently, and by accident.

He realised it could not be willed directly, but he asked himself,

Are there no technical means for the development of the creative state? This does not mean, of course, that I want to create inspiration by artificial means. No, that is impossible! I want to learn how to create, not inspiration itself, but rather, the conditions favourable for it; that state in which inspiration is more likely to enter our soul.

This was the starting point for the Stanislavski **"system"** of acting. He began to seek the means, the exercises, which could help to achieve the "creative state." He analysed the work of great actors, and saw in them a sense of physical freedom and relaxation when on stage.

When, for example, Salvini, as Othello, suffocated Desdemona, "his fingers touched her throat without the slightest tension, and the audience was struck with horror."

So, Stanislavski tried to achieve this sense of **relaxation**.

Watching a visiting star, he felt strongly that the actor's entire attention was on the stage. His focus was not on the audience, he was not distracted by the thousands of pairs of eyes fixed on him. Instead, he was completely absorbed in what he was doing.

Stanislavski realised that this increased his own interest in what was happening. He concluded that creativity on the stage demands the actor's complete **concentration** - mental, physical, and emotional.

Above all, perhaps, Stanislavski realised that the actor must *believe* in everything that takes place on the stage.

Every moment on stage must be filled with belief in the truthfulness of the emotion felt and the actions carried out.

Otherwise, the performance will be mechanical and empty. Without belief, it is impossible to *live* your role, "or to create anything ..."

But it is not easy for the actor to believe, when everything on stage is false: scenery, cardboard, paint, make-up, and props. How can you overcome this? Stanislavski suggested that the actor should say to him/herself,

If this was real, how would I react? What would I do?

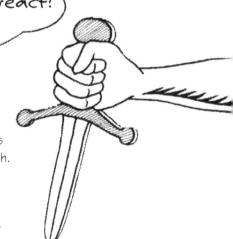

This question acts as a kind of key to open a door and let the actor enter the imaginative world of the play. It does not matter, then, if the actor playing Othello is given a cardboard dagger to kill himself with. What matters is the *inner feeling* of the actor, who can imagine how someone in Othello's shoes *would* have acted, *if* the circumstances were real, and *if* the dagger was made of metal.

In his book, *The Actor's Work on the Self*, Stanislavski (through the fictional persona of the director Tortsov) tells a story of how, at a party one evening, a group of friends decided to perform a mock operation on him. The "surgeons" put on white coats, and he was laid on the "operating table" and blindfolded. Suddenly the thought flashed through his mind,

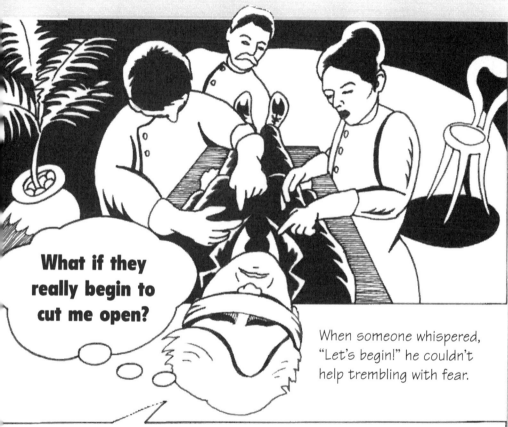

What if they really begin to cut me open?

When someone whispered, "Let's begin!" he couldn't help trembling with fear.

The question is: were the feelings I experienced true, was my belief in them real, or would it be more accurate to say it was the "verisimilitude of feeling"?

Stanislavski concluded: of course he knew it wasn't actually real; and yet, the experience awakened real feelings in him - **as if** it was real...

Stanislavski, then, was not looking for **"naturalistic"** truth on stage, the truth of everyday life. He was looking for an *inner* truth. Shchepkin said that you might act well, or you might act badly; but "you should always act truthfully." And to act "truthfully", in Stanislavski's view, meant to think, feel and act in unison with the character; to *live through* the role.

Earlier theoreticians of acting, such as Diderot and Coquelin, insisted that an actor does not "*live through*" the role. Acting was a case of finding the correct gestures to affect the audience, the "outward signs of feeling."

Diderot (1713 - 84) argued that the actor "feels neither trouble, nor sorrow, nor depression, nor weariness of soul. All these emotions he has given to you. The actor is tired, you are unhappy; he has had exertion without feeling, you feeling without exertion." This was his famous "paradox of acting."

DIDEROT

Similarly, the French actor, Constant Coquelin (1841 - 1909) insisted,

COQUELIN

The actor does not live, but "play." He remains cold towards the object of his acting, but his art must be perfect.

Stanislavski argued that acting void of feeling might be polished and effective, but would always remain empty, and...

Nothing can evoke a living, human response in the spectator more than the living, human emotion of the actor.

He maintained that there are three kinds of acting:

1. "Craft."

The "actor-craftsman" is not interested in "living the role," he just uses established methods, and ready-made clichés, to represent different feelings. The result "is a caricature of human emotion, which can only be laughed at."

2. The art of presenting a role

In this case, the actor tries to live through the role - but only at home, alone, or in rehearsal. Then, he or she works on finding an outer, physical form, which is then fixed. Actors of this type don't live through the role on stage. There is no genuine truth and belief and no real feeling in performance. There is "a split between body and soul."

3. The art of "experience" or "living through" (*perezhivanie*)

Acting, for Stanislavski, is not a question of "presenting" a role. The character must *live* on stage, not simply *appear* to exist.

The goal of the art of perezhivanie (living through) is to create the life of the human spirit and to show this life in an artistic scenic form.

The actor must create not only the conscious, but also the subconscious life of a role.

All the feelings, sensations and thoughts of the role must become the living, vibrant feelings, sensations and thoughts of the actor.

Stanislavski acknowledged that this is not easy, and in most performances, the trends he identified are mixed together: one moment the actor might "*live*" the role, and the next, only "*represent*" it.

KARATIGIN
AS HAMLET

Two famous Russian actors, contemporaries of Shchepkin, were held up as opposite types of actor. **Vassili Karatigin** (1802 - 1853) had a handsome appearance and a sonorous voice. His acting was highly polished and full of striking vocal and physical effects, but it was said that he did not put his heart into it; as a result he did not provoke strong emotions in the audience.

Pavel Mochalov (1800 - 1848), on the other hand, lacked technical skill, but was highly emotional and acted by inspiration. When he felt inspired, his acting was passionate and compelling; at other times, he was simply dull.

Stanislavski saw that actors often pin their hopes on "inspiration," trusting it will appear when needed. Indeed, some believed that an actor should rely on nothing else. But how can you hope to be "inspired," on cue, at 7.30 each night?

Stanislavski believed, in fact, that "nine-tenths of any genuine creative process" takes place subconsciously, intuitively; and "the most precious things about it are those flashes of unconscious inspiration."

MOCHALOV

But inspiration is rare, you have to be able to pin it down. Otherwise, the actor will play in an inspired way today and very feebly tomorrow...

But you cannot *force* the subconscious to work, or you'll destroy it. So Stanislavski sought the answer in an *oblique* instead of a *direct* approach. He looked for technical means, **conscious** steps, which could indirectly awaken the actor's natural, **subconscious** creativity. This, then, became the goal of his **"system"** :

The subconscious through the conscious.

He began to develop his ideas in practice. They were never carved in stone, but were constantly changing and evolving. Methods were tried and later discarded. However, the aim remained the same: the subconscious through the conscious.

[By the way, Stanislavski's notion of a "subconscious" had nothing to do with Freud - he didn't know Freud's work. He argued he was using terms such as "the subconscious" and "intuition" in their "simplest, everyday connotation," and not in any philosophical or psychoanalytical sense.]

After his Finnish holiday, Stanislavski began work on his next production, The Drama of Life by Knut Hamsun. He enlisted Leopold Sulerzhitski (known as Suler) as his personal assistant.

Suler was a painter and writer; a disciple of Leo Tolstoy. He was an important ally to Stanislavski as he worked on the "system"; indeed, Stanislavski declared that Suler was the only person who ever understood him fully.

SULER

Hamsun's play is a symbolist drama, which demanded "the passionate experience of abstract thoughts and feelings." Stanislavski focused on the inner life of the characters. He wanted the actors to live through their roles and achieve the maximum of inner feeling, with the minimum of external movement and gesture.

In this way, an eye movement, a raised hand, has acquired ten times more significance.

This demanded the actor's *complete concentration*.

Stanislavski realised, not for first or last time, that it is easy to dream and create theories, but harder to practise them. The actors tried to squeeze out emotion - but in fact, there was no real feeling. It lay hidden, frightened away by the forced attempts to arouse it. The approach was simply too direct. At one rehearsal, Suler even tried to get an actor to feel by sitting on his back, while the actor chewed the floor with emotion...

Again, again! Come on! More!

After this production, Stanislavski experienced months of despair. He knew he had to find more indirect methods, to develop the actors' inner technique.

Nevertheless, the staging was new, even revolutionary. In one scene, for example, the world was portrayed as a vision of Armageddon, with fantastic shadows writhing inside canvas booths. At the end of the performance, half of the audience cheered wildly and cried,

Death to realism!

All praise to our leading theatre!

Long live the left!

The other (more conservative) half exclaimed,

Shame on the Art Theatre!

Down with the decadents!

Long live the old theatre!

Stanislavski's next production also caused a sensation. He was always dissatisfied with the crudeness of theatrical settings made of canvas, glue, paint, papier-mache etc. They did not live up to the work of the artist/designer. Once, in a workshop, he lost a piece of black velvet. He searched everywhere without success - until he found it, hanging against another piece of black velvet. He had not been able to see it, because you cannot see black on black.

Stanislavski thought he had discovered a new and exciting principle of stage production. The whole stage could be covered in velvet. Against this backdrop, it would be possible to make furniture, props, even actors, appear and disappear as if by magic, simply by uncovering or covering them with velvet. The lingering showman in Stanislavski was attracted by the idea. He used it when he directed *The Life of Man* by Leonid Andreyev in 1907; it was called a "conception of genius." But Stanislavski later wrote off the production. The design was new - but again, there was nothing new in the acting. Moreover, the use of black velvet, he saw, was just a director's trick, a piece of theatrical hokum.

Stanislavski once said that theatre should stage fairy tales with a sense of "living truth." For his next production, he chose Maeterlinck's *The Blue Bird*, a fable about two children who set out on Christmas Eve to discover the blue bird of happiness. In his opening speech to the company, he urged the actors to cultivate a child-like faith and naïveté, a willingness to believe. The spectacular designs by Egorov were based on children's drawings, and audiences were enchanted by the production's magical beauty.

Stanislavski now felt the need to return to realism for a time, to continue his investigations into acting. In 1909, he staged A Month in the Country by Ivan Turgenev. He realised that he wanted to abandon director's tricks, and elaborate productions, to focus on the actor as the centre of the theatre.

There were no detailed mises en scène; all he wanted was a bench or a sofa, "at which people arrive, sit and speak; no sound effects, no details, no incidentals." Everything, he said, should be based on "simplicity and the inner delineation of the role." Again, he wanted to try to communicate "the inner essence" of feelings and ideas, with minimal movement. It was a return in some ways to the methods of The Drama of Life - applied now to a realistic comedy about Russian life.

STANISLAVSKI AS RAKITIN

A COOPER NATALYA PETROVNA

Great stress was placed on non-verbal communication between the actors - especially through the eyes. As early as 1904, Stanislavski had remarked,

When an actor begins to live in the role, his feelings will be reflected in his eyes, and if he can show them to the audience, they will read his emotions in them and will live through the feelings and thoughts of the character with him.

Now, he declared that what was needed was some sort of unseen emanation or "radiation" of the actors' emotions and desires, through the eyes, and through the subtlest changes in the face and voice.

As Stanislavski attempted to define the elements of his **"system,"** new terms began to appear, such as the **"circle of attention"** and **"adaptation."** There were exercises in concentration, to help the actor to forget the audience, and become absorbed in the action on stage.

In his production notebook, Stanislavski now no longer set down the actors' every move and gesture; instead, his notes hinted at the inner thoughts and emotional states of the characters. In rehearsal, he divided each role into segments, in order to show how the character's feelings develop, logically and in stages.

During rehearsals, he wrote:

Very interesting experiments are taking place... My system works wonders, and the whole company has gone for it.

However, the **"system"** was by no means fully accepted by everyone in the theatre. Nemirovich was hostile, and Stanislavski knew his ideas were on trial. The intensive work produced results in rehearsal - but when it came to acting for the first time on the main stage, suddenly everything seemed to disappear.

The enemies of my system were gloating, they said it was boring... It's long time since I've experienced such torture, despair and loss of energy.

But when the production opened, it was a success, and Stanislavski's performance was seen as exceptional.

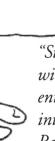

SMUG

NEWSPAPER REVIEW ↘

"Stanislavski plays Rakitin almost without gesture... Nevertheless, the entire external restraint, the economy of intonation and gesture, does not conceal Rakitin's emotional life. It is conveyed through the eyes."

Stanislavski was satisfied, less because of his own personal success, than because his ideas had been vindicated. Audiences could sense the difference in the company's acting.

In August, 1911 - much to everyone's surprise - Nemirovich suddenly announced that the "system" was now the official working method of the Art Theatre.

After a return to "realism" in A Month in the Country, Stanislavski felt the company was ready to set out again on the "road to discovery." Isadora Duncan had urged him to work with the English stage designer, Edward Gordon Craig.

Craig believed that the ideal actor was a puppet or Übermarionette in the hands of the director, so it was perhaps strange that Stanislavski would choose to collaborate with him. But he was excited by Craig's ideas for new, architectonic forms of stage design.

They agreed to produce Hamlet together. Craig designed a series of great screens, which could be arranged on stage in endless combinations. They hinted at buildings, streets, towers, etc. The screens would move smoothly between scenes, and in view of the audience, to form a new arrangement. With lighting, an infinite number of different moods could be created.

EDWARD GORDON CRAIG

(Actually, the screens proved difficult to make, and they didn't stand up very well. An hour before the first performance, one of them began to fall, and sent the others crashing to the ground like dominoes. The performance went ahead, but the plan to move the screens between scenes in full view of the audience had to be abandoned.)

Craig interpreted the play as a symbolist monodrama (in which events and other characters are shown only as the hero perceives them, as projections of his or her feelings). In the most spectacular scene, the King and Queen sat on a high golden throne. The courtiers all wore golden mantles - creating a sea of gold, which covered the stage. It was a dazzling image of the opulence and decadence of the court "as Hamlet sees it in his tormenting visions." Scenes like this made Simov declare that the production "literally staggered us and knocked us back on our heels."

Craig wanted the acting in *Hamlet* to convey "the white heat of emotion"; to achieve "that state which we have called ecstatic." He did not want false theatricality - but at the same time, he argued that if the acting was too "realistic," it would rob the play of poetry. One day, Stanislavski demonstrated different kinds of acting to him; but Craig didn't like any of them. At the same time, he could not explain what he wanted, or how to achieve it, except in the vaguest terms.

Stanislavski was convinced now that all forms of "*theatrical abstraction*" and "*stylisation*" needed to be based on a **"refined and intensified realism."**

All other ways are false and dead. That was proved by Meyerhold.

In rehearsal, he gave the work an *inner* realism, focusing on the characters' motives and desires. He was worried that the actors would fall into the trap of conventional verse-speaking - so he asked them to write the characters' desires next to the lines; this became the "score" of the role. In this way, they always had a *reason* for speaking.

Not a single sound on stage must be without meaning.

But while the company eschewed conventional theatricality, they did not find the "poetry" Craig hoped for. Kachalov's performance as Hamlet was praised for its naturalness ; but the actor himself was worried that it was boring. After the production, Stanislavski reflected that the company was able to apply the "system" with some success in modern plays, but "we had not found corresponding techniques to interpret sublime and heroic plays, and still had many years of immense and difficult work ahead of us."

It had taken some three years to produce Hamlet. (It was finally performed in December 1911.) It did not help that Stanislavski had caught typhoid fever in the middle of rehearsals (in the summer of 1910); but it was also true that he was taking longer and longer to stage plays. Nemirovich complained that he often turned valuable rehearsal time into acting lessons.

Stanislavski felt that his discoveries were in their early stages and already realised that the "system" could not be explained in an hour or a day; it had to be studied, systematically and practically, for years - for a lifetime.

You must reach the point when you stop thinking about it, when it appears naturally, by itself. It must become habitual, second nature to the actor.

He decided to create the First Studio, a centre for learning and experiment, where the "system" could be taught. It opened in 1912. Members were drawn from the Art Theatre; they had to fulfil their obligations to the main company, as well as attend classes, and rehearse plays when they could - often late into the night.

Suler was put in charge. In 1913, the Studio staged a production of *The Wreck of "The Hope"* by Herman Heijermans, and this was followed a year later by an adaptation of Dickens' story, *The Cricket and the Hearth*. The theatre space was intimate and so actors did not have to strain their voices and stress their acting theatrically. Partly because of this, Stanislavski thought,

In this production, perhaps for the first time, those deep and heartfelt notes of subconscious feeling could be heard, in the measure and form I dreamed of...

An important element in the "system" at the time was the concept of **affective memory**. This was inspired by Stanislavski's reading of the works of the French psychologist, Théodule-Armand Ribot (including **The Psychology of the Emotions** and **Diseases of the Will**). Here, he found the idea that experiences and emotions, like sights and sounds, leave traces in the memory. Sometimes these memories are revived in us quite spontaneously, and something of the original feeling returns ; but they can also be consciously evoked.

Exercises were developed to help the actor to tap into his or her store of affective memories, and release feelings analogous to their characters'. In *The Cricket on the Hearth*, Vera Solovyova as Bertha had problems in crying on command, so she used the affective memory of her own mother's death. It worked; after several performances, however, the power of this memory waned, and she had to seek other memories to create the same effect.

VERA SOLOVYOVA

Michael Chekhov (the playwright's nephew) was a member of the Studio. One day, as a class exercise, Chekhov "relived" the memory of his own father's funeral. Stanislavski was very moved, and embraced Chekhov - thinking the exercise again proved the power of affective memory. However, Stanislavski later discovered that Chekhov's father was in fact still very much alive... The young actor had simply used the power of his own imagination.

The concept of affective memory has, in fact, proved very controversial. And in later years, Stanislavski himself came to recognise that forcing emotions from memory could be dangerous, producing an inner hysteria in actors.

HEY! I'M ONLY ACTING!

MICHAEL CHEKHOV

In 1914, he began working on a revival of a production, first staged in 1906, of the Russian verse classic by Griboyedov, *Woe from Wit*. He played the role of Famusov. Then, between 1916 and 1920, he drafted notes on the play, which offer a picture of his methods at this time.

The process of creating a character must be done slowly, he insisted. He divided the work into three stages...

1. The period of discovery

After reading the play, the actor becomes acquainted with the character through a process of analysis. This does not mean dry, intellectual dissection. For an actor, Stanislavski argued, to know is to feel. The purpose of analysis is to help the actor to put feelings into the role.

In his notes, Stanislavski first

examines the facts of Griboyedov's play, or the "given circumstances." Then, he begins to use his imagination, to breathe life into these facts. He imagines the house in which the characters live ; and then he visualises the characters themselves, and starts to develop a sense of a relationship with them. He begins to feel part of the world of the play. Stanislavski calls this the state of "I am" - a sense of actually being in the situation and living through the circumstances of the play.

STANISLAVSKI AS FAMUSOV ('WOE FROM WIT', 1914)

2. The period of emotional experience or "living through" (perezhivanie)

If the first period explored the "given circumstances," then this second stage is intended to help the actor to *live through* the role.

"Action" on stage, Stanislavski argued, does not simply mean a lot of moving about. The actor must discover the *inner action*: the impulses and desires that motivate the character's behaviour.

Real life consists of a continuous succession of impulses, desires and aspirations, both big and small - from the desire to be a doctor or a teacher, to the desire to have a cup of tea. The actor must discover the desires, the *objectives* of the character. What does the character actually want?

Defining these objectives, moment by moment, scene by scene, establishes the "flow" of the character's inner life. It helps the actor to understand and *live through the role from within.*

It is important that these objectives should be believable ; they should engage the actor's own feelings, and stimulate the desire to carry them out. If they don't, they won't come to life.

Stanislavski focuses on the character of the hero in "Woe from Wit," Chatski, and defines his objectives in detail. This creates a "score" of the role, giving the actor a kind of pathway to follow, from moment to moment, through the whole play.

3. The period of physical embodiment

Now we have prepared our desires, objectives and aspirations, we can carry them out, not only internally, spiritually, but also externally, physically; using words and movements to convey our thoughts and feelings, or simply carrying out purely physical, external objectives: to walk, shake hands, move things, drink, eat, write - always with a goal.

Stanislavski imagines himself in Chatski's shoes. He finds that he begins to make gestures and movements not only consciously but also unconsciously, intuitively.

He begins to live the role.

It can be seen that at this stage, Stanislavski was working from the internal to the external. He argued that "action" on stage is, in fact,

...movement from the soul to the body, from the centre to the periphery, from the internal to the external, from emotional experiences to physical embodiment... External action on the stage, when it is not inspired, not justified, not called forth by internal action, is entertaining only for the eyes and ears ; it does not penetrate the soul, it has no significance for the life of the human spirit.

The actor's body must, however, be able to express the subtlest shades of subconscious feeling.

Alas for the actor if there is a split between body and soul, between feelings and words, between internal and external action and movements. Alas, if the actor's physical instruments falsify and distort the expression of feelings. It is like a melody played on an instrument which is out of tune. Moreover, the more truthful the feeling is, and the more spontaneous its expression, the more painful the dissonance and discord.

In 1915, Stanislavski played Salieri in Pushkin's tragedy, *Mozart and Salieri*. He felt he lived the role; but he was also painfully aware that his external technique - voice, movement, rhythm, etc., - was inadequate. This was torture for him; in despair he concluded:

It seemed my whole life had been lived in vain, as if I had learnt nothing, and had followed the wrong path in art.

Stanislavski's quest began again. He now placed an increased emphasis on developing external technique. For example, he began to analyse the **"laws of speech."**

An actor must know his or her own tongue to perfection. What use are all the subtleties of feeling (perezhivanie) if they are expressed on stage in poor speech?

The *internal* and the *external*, in fact, must be merged; there can be no "split" between the two.

On 17 December 1916, Suler died. Stanislavski was devastated. At the funeral, he wept bitterly, like a child.

In 1916, rehearsals began for *The Village of Stepanchikovo*. This was a new adaptation of the story by Dostoevsky, which Stanislavski had staged in 1891 as *Foma*. Now he was again playing Colonel Rostanev. When he played it before, he found the character intuitively; he *became* Rostanev. But he did not simply want to repeat himself. He began to apply the "system" to the play and role.

After 156 rehearsals, the production was still not ready, so Nemirovich took over. He tried to impose his own ideas of Rostanev on Stanislavski - but this made the actor angry and confused. He feared the result would be something dead, not living.

At the dress rehearsal, Stanislavski stood in the wings in tears. Immediately afterwards, Nemirovich removed him from the cast, and replaced him with Massalitinov. He said that Stanislavski had failed to bring the part to life. This devastated Stanislavski. He declared:

I shall never act in a new play again.

He kept to his word. Apart from a part in *Tsar Fyodor* which he played during a foreign tour (when Nemirovich wasn't around!), he never again created a new role.

Act V: Stanislavski and the State

The Second Revolution in Russia occurred in February 1917; the Tsar was forced to abdicate and a Provisional Government was formed. Then, on the night of the 25th of October, the Bolshevik uprising began in St. Petersburg.

On the 26th of October, the Art Theatre performed *The Cherry Orchard*. There was an air of tension in Moscow, and soldiers were massing outside the Kremlin. Yet, at this revolutionary time, the theatre was performing a play that sympathetically portrayed the life of the landed gentry, the very class the Revolution was directed against. The actors backstage were worried they wouldn't be able to finish the performance. "They'll drive us off the stage," they said.

In fact, the audience sat spellbound. It was as if, Stanislavski said, they wanted to wrap themselves up in the play's atmosphere, and say farewell to the old life forever. The performance ended with a tremendous ovation.

Stanislavski was never very politically aware; but it seems he welcomed the Revolution - although it meant the family business was taken into state ownership, and his personal fortune was lost. He always believed that theatre should have a social and educational function. Now he saw the Revolution as the opportunity to spread knowledge and enlightenment. New audiences were flooding to the theatre ; and they came "expecting something important, something they had never seen before."

During the Civil War that followed the Revolution (between the **"Reds"** and the counter-revolutionary **"Whites"**), there was severe economic hardship ; but Stanislavski argued that art must be preserved. He declared:

Theatre for the starving! Starvation and Theatre! There is no contradiction here. Theatre is not a luxury in the life of the people, but a necessity.

The years following the Revolution saw an explosion of theatrical activity, and experiments in new forms such as futurism and constructivism, but the Art Theatre itself seemed to be stagnating. Stanislavski feared it had lost its purpose and direction. There were rumours that it would be forced to close. The company had split in two when a group of actors, touring in the Ukraine, were cut off from Moscow by the Civil War. This included Kachalov and Knipper. They were only reunited with the main company in 1922. Partly as a result, between 1917 and 1922 the theatre staged only one new production, Byron's *Cain*. This biblical drama was a strange choice for this revolutionary era, and the play only lasted for eight performances. The repertoire was stuck in the past, and the company was increasingly attacked as outmoded and even "counter-revolutionary." The critic Vladimir Blyum said that it represented the best in Russian bourgeois culture - but it had died a natural death on the night of the October Revolution, when the bourgeois class was overthrown.

Some left-wing critics, indeed, wanted to see the abolition of all "pre-Revolutionary" art. But Lenin said,

If there is one theatre from the past, which we must save and preserve - it is, of course, the Art Theatre!

It was given the official status of a State Academic theatre in 1919.

LENIN

In 1918, Stanislavski was asked to work with the Bolshoi Opera, to help singers to develop as actors. He agreed to form a Studio for young artists. He wanted to show that a singer must also be an actor, and live through the role.

Stanislavski himself in his early years had hoped to become an opera singer, but his voice was not strong enough. He had trained with **Fyodor Komissarzhevski** (one of the co-founders of the Society of Art and Literature), and together they explored the idea of movement in rhythm.

Now in the Opera Studio, Stanislavski's interest in rhythm was renewed. The focus was not only on the rhythm of outward movement, but also - and more importantly - on *inner* rhythm.

There is a *"tempo"* and a *"rhythm"* in everything we do. You experience quite a different tempo-rhythm when you are sunbathing on a beach, than when you are waiting for a job interview.

A sense of tempo-rhythm on stage, Stanislavski argued, makes you act and even breathe differently. This was an important development in the Stanislavski **"system"**; in his work with actors, he increasingly emphasised the need to find the right *tempo-rhythm* for every moment in a scene.

On March 5, 1921, Stanislavski was given a new home at 6 Leontyevski Lane. On the first floor, there was a large ballroom that Stanislavski determined to use for "chamber" productions by the Opera Studio, beginning with *Eugene Onegin* in 1922. Stripping the opera of clichés, Stanislavski created a real sense of the world in which the characters lived. In rehearsal, he stressed the need for the singers to put meaning into every word. There were no "artificial histrionics." Anatoli Lunacharski sensed an affinity between the rhythm of the music, and the inner rhythm of the actors.

It was a legendary production, and the ballroom at Leontyevski Lane subsequently became known as the Onegin Room.

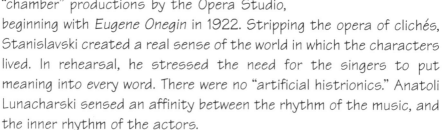

In 1921, the First Studio staged Strindberg's *Erik XIV*, directed by Evgeni Vakhtangov. Vakhtangov was one of Stanislavski's pupils. He joined the Art Theatre in 1911, and began to act and teach in the Studio. In fact, Stanislavski declared that he could "teach my system better than I can"; he even asked Vakhtangov to coach *him* in his own "system," when he was working on the role of Salieri...

MICHAEL CHEKHOV IN 'ERIK XIV'

In the aftermath of the Revolution, and perhaps influenced by the views of left-wing critics, Vakhtangov began to distance himself from his mentor - at least in private. He said that "Stanislavski's theatre is dead and will never be reborn." When he staged *Erik XIV*, he wrote :

Up to now, the studio, true to Stanislavski's teaching, has doggedly aimed for the mastery of inner experience "perezhivanie". Now the studio is entering a period of search for new forms...

He wanted a vivid and *theatrical* style of performance - or, as he termed it, **"imaginative realism."** In the search for "new forms," he became interested in the concept of the "grotesque," which he defined as acting which went beyond "*realism*" into new realms of fantasy and exaggeration. In *Erik XIV*, non-naturalistic make-up was used to create a sense of the "grotesque."

Stanislavski debated the concept with Vakhtangov and later recorded their conversation. He argued he had seen few real "grotesque" performances in his time (Salvini's *Othello* was one example). The "grotesque" does not mean *external* exaggeration with no *internal* justification.

No, a real grotesque is the outward, most vivid and bold justification of a tremendous inner content, exhaustive to the point of exaggeration. An actor must not only feel and live through human passions in all their component elements - they must be condensed and made visible, irresistible in their expressiveness, audacious and bold, bordering on caricature.

Simply sticking a crooked eyebrow on an actor's face (as Vakhtangov did in *Erik XIV*) does not create the "grotesque."

To inflate something, which is not there, to inflate emptiness - that makes me think of blowing soap bubbles.

This did not imply a rejection of "theatricality," but only of a false theatricality. "New forms" cannot simply be imposed on the actor.

In productions such as *The Government Inspector* (the 1921 revival), *The Burning Heart* (1926), and *Dead Souls* (1932), Stanislavski demonstrated his approach to the "grotesque." The performances were heightened and exaggerated, yet based on internal truth, on a "refined and intensified" inner realism. This was the "life of the human spirit," expressed in an "artistic scenic form."

Vakhtangov's final production was Gozzi's fairy tale, *Princess Turandot* (1922). It was a dazzling theatrical spectacle with a sense of an almost childlike spontaneity and naïvety in the performances. Vakhtangov, ill with cancer, could not attend the final dress rehearsal. In one of the intervals, Stanislavski rushed to his apartment to congratulate him.

It's a resounding success. Your young actors have matured considerably...

Did you believe them? I always demand that they really live on the stage - cry, laugh...

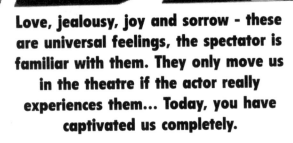

Love, jealousy, joy and sorrow - these are universal feelings, the spectator is familiar with them. They only move us in the theatre if the actor really experiences them... Today, you have captivated us completely.

Three months later, Vakhtangov died.

The leading figure in the "search for new forms" in post-revolutionary Russia was Vsevolod Meyerhold. Every new production by him was a major event. He did not want to create the illusion of real life on the stage but to celebrate the "theatricality" of theatre. In his production of *The Magnanimous Cuckold* (1922), he experimented with **"constructivism"** - replacing "realistic" sets with functional constructions or "machines" for acting. The actors wore loose overalls rather than costumes.

Meyerhold declared that the production "was meant to establish the basis for a new style of acting." He rejected the need for realistic

A 'MACHINE FOR ACTING'

character "psychology" and "authentic emotions." Instead, he said that the actor's art is the art of gesture and movement, or "plastic forms in space." The performances in *The Magnanimous Cuckold* were physical, even acrobatic. Movement was synchronised and rhythmic.

But when Stanislavski saw the production, it did not seem very revolutionary to him. He thought it should be even bolder in its theatricality. "I've been doing all that for a long time!" he said. (Presumably, he meant the kind of experiment in rhythmic movement, which was evident in his work as early as the 1887 production of *The Mikado*.)

Stanislavski and Meyerhold have been portrayed as theatrical opposites: one concerned with inner "content," the other with external "form"; one celebrating "truth of feeling," the other "theatricality." But this is simplistic.

Meyerhold was one of the Art Theatre's most persistent critics, though he continued to profess his admiration for Stanislavski personally. "I am Stanislavski's pupil," he declared ; and Stanislavski called him his "prodigal son." Meyerhold observed:

The assertion that Meyerhold and Stanislavski are antipodes is wrong. This notion is meaningless in such an ossified and static form. Neither Stanislavski nor Meyerhold represents something completed. Both are in a constant process of change.

When Meyerhold saw Stanislavski's production of *The Burning Heart*, he said that his own young company "could not even dream of the brilliant skill shown today at the Art Theatre." Stanislavski much admired Meyerhold's production of *The Warrant* (1925): he said that in the third act, Meyerhold had achieved "what I have dreamed of" : a sense of the "genuine grotesque." In later years, Meyerhold concluded that the two men were ultimately working towards the same goal: combining the actor's creativity, with the demands of theatrical form. They were:

... like the builders of a tunnel under the Alps: he is coming from one side, and I from the other, but somewhere in the middle, inevitably, we must meet.

In 1922, the Art Theatre began a new tour abroad, to Europe and America - partly in order to raise much-needed income; but it also gave the company the chance to regroup, and reflect on its future.

When they sailed into New York in January 1923, they were greeted with suspicion in some quarters; indeed, before their arrival, the American Defence Society protested against the visit, declaring that the company were Soviet spies and would use profits from the tour to promote World Communism.

One reporter asked Stanislavski, "Why did you choose these particular plays to include in your repertoire? I mean *Tsar Fyodor*, *The Lower Depths* and Chekhov's plays?"

I understood immediately the hidden meaning behind the question, because I remembered what had been said and written in Europe - that we had chosen Tsar Fyodor to show a weak tsar, The Lower Depths to demonstrate the strength of the proletariat, and Chekhov's plays to illustrate the feebleness of the intelligentsia and the bourgeoisie.

He told the reporter:

We've brought the plays we were asked to bring, and no others. They were asked for because they are the most typical of an earlier period of the Art Theatre, and because we performed them in Europe in 1906 and just recently. And America wants to see what Europe already knows.

The tour was a sensational success and left a lasting influence on American acting.

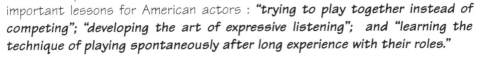

'LOWER DEPTHS'

Critics and audiences were deeply impressed by the strong sense of ensemble playing, and the truthfulness of the performances. Diana Bourbon pointed out three important lessons for American actors : **"trying to play together instead of competing"; "developing the art of expressive listening"; and "learning the technique of playing spontaneously after long experience with their roles."**

The choice of repertoire, however, concentrating on the Art Theatre's early successes, created a *misleading* view of Stanislavski's work. The company became forever associated in people's minds with a form of "poetic naturalism," seen mostly clearly in Chekhov's plays. When, in 1965, the Art Theatre returned to the States, critics were surprised by the bold and theatrical performance style in Stanislavski's production of *Dead Souls*; it confounded all their expectations and preconceptions.

'TSAR FYODOR'

RICHARD BOLESLAVSKI

American theatre practitioners wanted to know more about Stanislavski's methods. **Richard Boleslavsky** had been an actor and director with the Art Theatre; he appeared in *A Month in the Country* and directed *The Wreck of "The Hope"* at the First Studio. He emigrated after the Revolution, and he was in New York to greet his former colleagues when they arrived in 1923. Articles by him about the Stanislavski "system" appeared in magazines, and they were later assembled in the book, *Acting: The First Six Lessons*. In 1924, he founded the American Laboratory Theatre. Among its early members were **Stella Adler**, **Harold Clurman** and **Lee Strasberg**. Adler said :

> **It was marvellous training. It was thorough and complete, well rounded and systematic, at an unmatchable level. And remember, we all had the recent model of the Moscow Art Theatre players to goad us, and to inspire us.**

STELLA ADLER

The programme included work in affective and sense memory. Clurman said that this was "the element that most excited many of the Lab's actors" - it was so novel.

In 1931, Clurman, Lee Strasberg and Cheryl Crawford founded The Group Theatre. From the beginning, Strasberg hoped to develop a shared approach to acting in the company, through improvisation, and through exercises in affective memory.

LEE STRASBERG

HAROLD CLURMAN

CHERYL CRAWFORD

Clurman recalled:

The first effect on the actors was that of a miracle... Here at last was a key to that elusive ingredient of the stage, true emotion. And Strasberg was a fanatic on the subject of true emotion. Everything was secondary to it.

PHOEBE BRAND

But more than one actor with the Group came to resist this emphasis on affective memory. Phoebe Brand said :

I lent myself to it for a while - it is valuable for a young actor to go through it, but it is too subjective. It makes for a moody, personal, self-indulgent acting style. It assumes an actor is an emotional mechanism that can just be turned on. Emotion can't be worked for in that way - it is rather a result of truthful action in given circumstances. Lee insisted on working each little moment of affective memory ; we were always going backwards into our lives. It was painful to dig back... Lee crippled a lot of people.

Another actor, Margaret Barker, recalled how Strasberg, to prepare her for a role in *The House of Connelly* (1931), made her go over and over a painful experience - "my roommate had been killed the year before - until I thought I was going to crack."

In 1934 Stella Adler met Stanislavski in Paris and told him that in using the "Method" she had stopped enjoying her acting. She did not like affective memory at all: "I said I thought it was sick." He replied:

If my System doesn't help you, don't use it ... but perhaps you're not using it correctly.

Stanislavski told her that he now only used affective memory when all else failed. He stressed, instead, the importance of *action*, and creating a *score* of the character's *objectives*.

When she had learnt this, she acted so brilliantly that we absolutely "howled" with delight.

Adler returned to the States and shared what she had learnt with the Group. Strasberg's response was unequivocal.

Stanislavski said we're doing it wrong.

Stanislavski doesn't know. I know.

The debate led to a historic split. Adler continued to oppose affective memory, which she maintained induced hysteria.

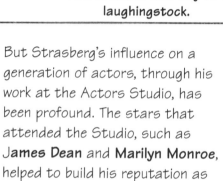

It's polluted water, and yet Americans, typically, continue to drink it. Stanislavski himself went beyond it. He was like a scientist conducting experiments in a lab; and his new research superseded his earlier ideas: the affective memory belonged to the older, worn-out ideas. But Lee always thought it was the cornerstone of the Method, and in this way he became a laughingstock.

But Strasberg's influence on a generation of actors, through his work at the Actors Studio, has been profound. The stars that attended the Studio, such as **James Dean** and **Marilyn Monroe**, helped to build his reputation as the guru of the American "Method."

In fact, our understanding of Stanislavski has been warped by Strasberg's teachings. We now tend to associate the **"system"** with a particular style of acting - *"moody, personal, self-indulgent"* - seen at its best in the work of actors such as **Marlon Brando**. But this has very little to do with Stanislavski.

MARILYN MONROE

JAMES DEAN

MARLON BRANDO

TOVSTONOGOV

The Russian director, Georgi Tovstonogov, once attended some of Strasberg's classes. He observed that Strasberg

... is considered a famous pupil of Stanislavski and I would have believed that if I hadn't seen those lessons myself. But in actuality everything he did was in complete opposition to Stanislavski: building on mood and atmosphere, demanding an emotional state all the time. That's just what Stanislavski fought against. Strasberg took all of Stanislavski's terminology... but he didn't possess the essence of Stanislavski at all.

After some two years abroad, Stanislavski finally returned to Moscow in August 1924. Some of the company remained in America. The tour had only postponed and not resolved the theatre's problems. Nemirovich, who had stayed behind in Russia, continued to worry about its role. What would it be like in future?

This question, this momento mori, is becoming ever more urgent, acute and frightening... What plays should we put on? Who should act in them? How should they act in them?

Part of problem was that the Art Theatre did not have a single play about the Revolution in its repertoire.

Nemirovich decided to reorganise the company. Students from the Second Studio, which had been created in 1916, were drawn into the main theatre. Stanislavski was now concerned that the older generation of actors, and the younger actors from the Studio, should blend into an ensemble. But some of the older actors were suspicious - and the younger members were looking for an opportunity to prove themselves...

Their chance came in a production of *The Days of the Turbins*, by **Mikhail Bulgakov**. The play was given them as an "experimental" production. It is set at the time of the Civil War, and follows the fortunes of the Turbin family, supporters of the "White" cause, as they wait out their last days before the victory of the "Reds." It is a realistic portrait of a way of life that had so recently vanished. It does not caricature the "White" forces, as Soviet plays of the period usually did ; instead, the characters are portrayed sympathetically, with all their strengths and weaknesses.

Between 1925-8, Stanislavski was responsible for nine productions at the Art Theatre. They were usually assigned to young directors supervised by him; he then reworked the results. After seeing a run-through, he would give his comments, thanking the company, and noting the things he liked. Everyone would wait for the "But" - which could mean, "Scrap the whole thing and start again..."

The Days of the Turbins was directed by **Ilya Sudakov**. On 26 March, 1926, there was a run-through for Stanislavski. As he watched, he seemed to "live through" every moment: he sat laughing and crying, biting his hand and throwing down his pince-nez in his excitement. Afterwards, he said, "Well, you could perform it tomorrow."

In fact, the first performance was on October 5. At the end, some in the audience cried out "Nonsense! Counter-revolutionaries!" while others said, "Thanks for the truth!" The theatre's left-wing critics were outraged by a play that seemed to support the White cause. Out of 301 reviews, Bulgakov counted 298 hostile ones. But Turbins was popular with audiences. The emotional impact of scenes such as the death of Aleksei Turbin was so great that hysteria and fainting in the audience were common, and a first aid team had to be on standby.

The morning after the premiere, the young actors in the play woke up famous. They came to see *Days of the Turbins* as the *Seagull* of their generation. But in 1929, it was banned. The story goes - and it may be apocryphal - that three years later, there was a call to the Art Theatre from Stalin's secretary : "Stalin wants to know when *Days of the Turbins* will be playing." The Great Leader liked the play and had seen it a number of times. The manager said the play had been taken out of the repertory. Within minutes, Stalin himself called and said,

Today is Tuesday; I will come to see this play on Saturday; put it back in the repertoire.

DIARY

EXECUTIONS

PLAYS & BOOKS TO BE BANNED

The theatre worked frantically to reassemble the cast and sets in time. With Stalin's blessing, the play stayed in rep for the next nine years.

Stanislavski followed *The Days of the Turbins* with *The Marriage of Figaro* by Beaumarchais (1927). This was one of his most famous productions. During rehearsal, he said that every scene should "sparkle like champagne" and "pulsate with rhythm and tempo." The colourful designs by Aleksandr Golovin helped to turn the evening into a festive celebration of theatre. One spectator wrote to Stanislavski: "All around us there is monotony and tedium, but in your production of *The Marriage of Figaro* everything is radiant and light, joyful and alive. One is amazed above all by this sense of the joy of life..."

Armoured Train 14-69 by Vsevolod Ivanov was chosen to mark the tenth anniversary of the October Revolution. Compared with *Days of the Turbins*, it is a much more conventional "Soviet" play. It shows the capture of an armoured train from counter-revolutionary forces. The central character begins as a peasant farmer and ends a hero of the Revolution. The Whites are portrayed as sadists and fools.

Playgoers at the time thought that, through this production, the Art Theatre was trying to prove its loyalty to the Soviet Union, and atone for *Turbins*. During rehearsal, the company was forced to make a number of changes to the script, and Stanislavski reported to his wife that...

Armoured Train has been half-banned. Pity they didn't ban it completely.

On the thirtieth anniversary of the theatre (27 October 1928), Stanislavski made a speech, in which he thanked the Government for allowing the Art Theatre to come to an understanding of the Revolution in its own way, and its own time.

Any other way would have pushed us into pseudo-revolutionary hackwork.

In an apparent reference to the campaign that had been waged against Bulgakov, he declared:

We must be patient and show good will, otherwise the most talented writers will be frightened off or pushed aside.

Two days later, there was a gala evening to mark the theatre's jubilee. Extracts were performed from past productions, including Act One of *Three Sisters*, with Stanislavski as Vershinin. During the performance, he felt sharp pains in his chest. Somehow he managed to carry on to the end, but then collapsed. A doctor diagnosed an attack of angina pectoris.

It was the last time he appeared on stage.

Act VI: The "System" Triumphant

Stanislavski had to spend several months in bed. In May 1929 he left Russia for a rest cure, travelling to Badenweiler in the Black Forest, and then to Nice. He did not return to Moscow until the autumn of 1930. He had contemplated writing a book about his acting methods for some years; now he began assembling his notes. The book that slowly (very slowly) emerged was called *The Actor's Work on the Self*. It is in two parts :

Part One : The Actor's Work on the Self in the Creative Process of "Living Through"
"perezhivanie" (The title is a bit of a mouthful and the book first appeared in America and the U.K. as "An Actor Prepares")

Part Two : The Actor's Work on the Self in the Creative Process of Physical Embodiment *(First published as "Building a Character")*

The first part concentrates on the actor's inner or *psycho*-technique, and is designed to help the actor to *live* the role.

The second part concentrates on physical work - movement, voice etc - and is intended to help the actor to express the inner life of the role in an "artistic, scenic form."

The two parts should be read together.
In fact, the plan was to publish them as one volume. The decision was made to split them into two separate books because of length.

The books appeared with a 14-year gap between them in the States - and a 17-year gap in the Soviet Union. This has had very unfortunate consequences. The first volume, inevitably, made more impact. There has even been an assumption that it *is* the "system." But it is only part of it. The second volume, focusing on physical work, has received comparatively little attention. Partly as a result some people have even assumed, quite erroneously, that the "system" is only concerned with the actor's *internal* technique, to the neglect of physical work.

The ideas are presented in the form of a fictional "diary" written by a young student, Kostya, who is studying acting with the director, Tortsov. Stanislavski chose this format because he did not want to use a "dry, scientific language"; instead, he wanted the book to be accessible to actors, and to work through concrete anecdotes and practical examples.

Both Kostya and Tortsov are loosely based on Stanislavski himself. Kostya represents Stanislavski in his youth - naïve and keen to learn. Tortsov represents the mature Stanislavski - the experienced director, teacher, and actor.

Trying to force emotion

X

"LET GO"

✓

Letting it come naturally

THE ACTOR'S WORK ON THE SELF (Part One)

The book opens with an actor finding "inspiration" on stage quite by chance. Kostya is preparing a scene from "Othello." On the day of the performance, he only feels empty inside; the "excessive effort to squeeze out the emotion" and "the powerlessness to achieve the impossible" produces tension in his whole body, paralysing his movements. But then the line, "O blood, blood, blood!" seems to burst from him, like "the frantic cry of a man in pain." It is a moment of real inspiration. He is acting "subconsciously, intuitively."

At the end of the first book, Kostya again experiences "inspiration" on the stage - but this time it is not by accident. Instead, he applies different elements of the actor's psycho-technique he has studied under Tortsov. He creates the conditions for "inspiration" to appear.

Action

The first lesson Tortsov's students learn is that everything that happens on the stage must happen for **a purpose**. One of them is asked to imagine she has lost a very valuable brooch, and must search for it. At first, she rushes around the stage, clutching her head or beating her breast in despair. But she actually forgets all about looking for the brooch itself...

Tortsov asks her to repeat the exercise - this time, concentrating on her **purpose**: to find the brooch. Her search now is painstaking and slow ; she is completely absorbed in her task; and the sincerity of her feelings is evident. Tortsov concludes: "Do not run for the sake of running, or suffer for the sake of suffering. On stage, you must not act in a 'generalised' way, for the sake of action; you must act with a purpose."

"Pretending" to look for something

"Really" looking for it

All too often, actors aim for results and try to show jealousy or despair and so on. The actor should remember that feelings are the result of something that has gone before. Rather than thinking about the feeling directly, the actor should concentrate on the steps that lead to it.

The Russian actor and director, **Iosif Rapoport** (who appeared in Vakhtangov's *Princess Turandot*), offered the following example. You cannot act "sorrow," but you might, say, be acting a scene in which someone you are close to is seriously ill. "You want to help him, ease his suffering, but you are unable to do so. Here is your task, fulfil it, fight for the person's health, do this in all sincerity - and you will evoke the authentic stage feeling which corresponds to the feeling we call sorrow."

In other words, the actor should concentrate on the **action** - on trying to achieve an **objective**. The action, in fact, will create the feeling.

"As If"

In working on a role, you should ask yourself : what would I *do if* I was in this situation? This helps to put you in the character's shoes: "*as if* acts as a lever, lifting us from the plane of reality, into the world where it is possible to create" - the world of imagination. "As if" does not ask you to believe something is real. Everyone knows it isn't. You simply act *as if* you were in these circumstances.

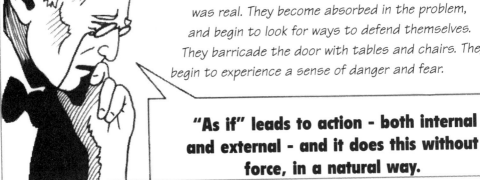

Tortsov's students do an improvisation. They are gathered on a stage set representing someone's apartment. They are asked to imagine that a man who used to live in the apartment became violently insane, and he was put in hospital; but now, Tortsov asks, "if he escaped, and he was standing outside that door, what would you do?" The students act as if this was real. They become absorbed in the problem, and begin to look for ways to defend themselves. They barricade the door with tables and chairs. They begin to experience a sense of danger and fear.

"As if" leads to action - both internal and external - and it does this without force, in a natural way.

Given Circumstances

The Great Russian writer, Aleksandr Pushkin, declared:

Sincerity of emotions, feelings that seem true in the given circumstances - that is what we demand from a dramatist.

And Stanislavski adds that this is also "exactly what we demand from the actor." What are the *given circumstances*? They are all the factors that an actor must take into account as he or she creates a character.

Firstly, there are the facts and events that happen in the play. The time and setting can also affect the way the characters think and behave, and their ways of relating to each other. The actor needs, moreover, to be aware of all the elements of the *mises en scène*, such as the set and lighting.

As *If* and the *given circumstances* work together: you imagine what you might do *if* you were in a particular situation.

Imagination

The actor needs imagination. The dramatist cannot supply everything that the actors need to know about the characters. There may be little information in the script about what has happened before the play begins. In the stage-directions, you might read the instruction, "Enter Peter" or "Exit Peter." But you need to know where you are coming from or where you are going to. The actor has to fill out the given circumstances with his or her imagination, otherwise there are gaps or blanks in the life of the role. (Preparing a revival of *Tsar Fyodor*, for example, Stanislavski told the actors to prepare answers to a whole series of questions: "Who am I?" "How old am I?" "What is my profession?" "Where do I live in Moscow?" "How did I spend yesterday?" and so on.)

If you say a single word, or do anything on stage mechanically, without knowing who you are, where you have come from, why, what you want, where you are going and what you will do when you get there - you will be acting without imagination, and this part of your time on stage, be it long or short, will not be truthful for you - you will be like a clockwork machine, an automaton.

Concentration of attention

The actor's attention on stage can tend to be scattered. In particular you can be all too aware of the audience, instead of concentrating on the stage, and the other people in a scene. To facilitate the actor's concentration, Stanislavski introduces the concept of...

Circles of attention

The student Kostya sits at a table. A single lamp throws a small circle of light. The rest of the stage is swallowed up in darkness. This represents a small "circle of attention." Kostya's whole attention is absorbed in the objects on the table. He even feels entirely alone, and more at home than in his own apartment. Tortsov calls this the state of **public solitude** - you are in public, and yet you feel alone, because your attention is not on other people, but concentrated within your own

"circle." "During a performance, before a crowd of thousands, you can always withdraw into this circle, like a snail into its shell."

A medium Circle is represented by a spotlight, which illuminates a fairly large area. "It was impossible to take in the whole space at once," Kostya says. "It was necessary to examine it bit by bit." Then, the whole stage is lit up, representing a large Circle.

Finally, adjoining rooms are lit up to depict the very largest Circle. If you were standing on a seashore, this Circle would be limited only by the horizon.

As the circle grows larger, so the area of your concentration must stretch. However, it is much harder to concentrate on the larger circles; as soon as your attention begins to waver, "you must quickly withdraw to a smaller circle," and begin to build your concentration again.

Relaxation

Physical tension impairs an actor's work. It hampers movements and constricts the voice. You need to relax your muscles on stage, not only in calm moments, but also in moments of the highest nervous and dramatic intensity. You have to be able to monitor yourself, and remove areas of unnecessary tension when they occur. This process of self-observation "must be developed to the point where it becomes an automatic, unconscious habit."

In all acting, relaxation is enhanced if you think of a *purpose* to your actions; *as if* you are in a particular situation. For example, if you are stretching a hand above your head, the action is simply mechanical and empty; but imagine you are reaching to pick a peach from a branch. The movement immediately becomes "a real action" with a living objective: to pick a peach. If you feel the truthfulness of this simple action, then you will find that superfluous tension disappears quite naturally.

Units

It is not possible to grasp a whole play or role at once. So, the actor must, in rehearsal, break a play down into smaller sections or "units."

What constitutes a "unit"? How do you define it?

Kostya walks home. He tries to break his journey down into units - going down the stairs, opening the door, stopping to look in a bookshop, etc. He ends up thoroughly confused, with more than two hundred tiny "units." But Tortsov points out that in fact the journey should be seen simply as one single, large unit, called **going home.**

To define a unit, look for where a new *action* begins - and where it ends. Kostya's journey, for example, began when he set

off, and ended when his goal was achieved; it formed a completed action.

Stanislavski suggests you need to find a *title* that captures the essence of each unit. This should not be a "literary" title such as **"A Mother's Love."** For each unit, you should ask yourself: "What happens?" Define the *action*, not the subject matter. (Thus, when he was working on Molière's *Tartuffe*, Stanislavski broke the play into units, and gave
them titles which sum up the action - e.g.,
"Protest against the oppression of Tartuffe,"
"Battle of two giants - Tartuffe and Elmire," etc.

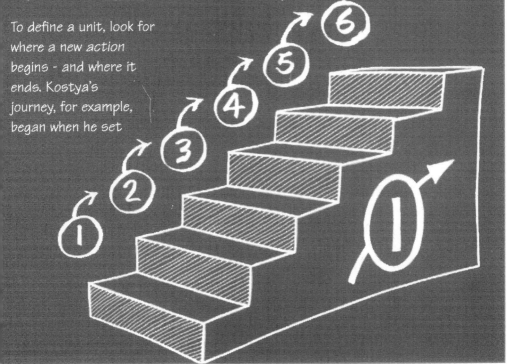

Objectives

In every unit, Stanislavski argues, "there is a *creative objective*" - a purpose, a goal. Kostya, for example, has a clear and simple objective: *to go home.*

Therefore, you need to define your character's objective in each unit.

As we have seen, an objective should be believable, and should make you want to carry it out. It should be defined using the phrase : *I want to...* (e.g. "I want to go home"). This suggests immediately the need, the desire for *action.*

The wording needs to be carefully thought out. *I want power,* for example, is too general. You must have something more concrete to do. You might say: "I want to do so and so, to obtain power."

Stanislavski distinguishes between a simple, ordinary task - such as entering a room and greeting someone... and greeting them in such a way as to show them your love, respect, or thanks. This action contains a psychological element.

If you are entering a room, in order to shakes hands with an enemy of yesterday - that is an even more complex task, and you would have to think carefully and overcome many emotions before you could do it. "This," Stanislavski concludes, "is what might be termed a psychological objective."

Every *physical* action, in fact, contains a psychological element - and vice versa: every *psychological* action has a physical component. The two things cannot be separated.

Tortsov advises his young actors to limit themselves at first to simple, physical objectives, rather than trying to play complex psychological objectives at once. Physical objectives, in fact, are "more available and easier to accomplish. Working through them, you reduce the risk of falling into artificiality."

He uses the example of Salieri in Pushkin's play, "Mozart and Salieri." The psychology of the character, as he plans Mozart's murder, is very complex. It is difficult for him to decide to take a glass, pour wine into it, add the poison, and give the glass to his friend... "These are all physical actions, and yet they contain so much psychology! Or, rather : these are complex psychological actions, and yet, they contain so much that is physical !"

When you have divided a role into units, and defined the character's objective in each unit, you have a kind of channel or pathway through the play.

You should not break a play down into too many small units. "The larger and fewer the units, the easier it is for you, with their help, to grasp the play and role as a whole." The division into units, moreover, must only be temporary; the play must not remain in fragments. It is only in the preparation of a role that small units are used. You break it down - and then reassemble it again, fusing the units together.

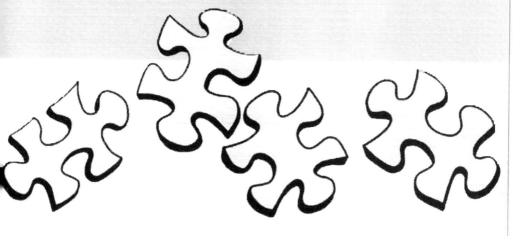

Faith and a sense of truth

Stanislavski believed that "every moment on stage must be filled with belief in the truthfulness of the emotion felt and the actions carried out." Truth in the theatre is sometimes confused with "naturalism."
Stanislavski argues:

Truth on the stage is whatever we can believe in sincerely, whether in ourselves, or in the souls of our partners. Truth is inseparable from belief, and belief - from truth. They cannot exist without each other, and without both of them, it is impossible to live through your role, or create anything.

Everything "must become real in the imaginative life of the actor." This does not mean that the play has to be "naturalistic" or "true to life." A play like *The Blue Bird*, for example, is a fairy tale that demands that the actor must believe in everything that happens, no matter how fantastical and unrealistic.

Tortsov sets the student actors a melodramatic situation to enact. He tells them : don't try to believe it all at once : "Attempt to master this difficult exercise bit by bit, working from the simplest physical actions, of course."

Kostya begins by simply counting an imaginary pile of bank notes. When he really believes in this, he begins to feel at ease on the stage.

"Truth" for Stanislavski is not some "general" concept, it is concrete. It must be based on belief in the smallest action.

If you can't grasp at once the truth of the larger action, then you must divide it into parts, and try to believe even if only in the smallest of them ... Perhaps you do not yet realise that, often from just one small moment of truth, from one moment of faith in the authenticity of an action, an actor can immediately begin to feel himself in his part and to believe in the greater truth of the whole play.

Emotion Memory

We have already seen the controversy that surrounds the concept of *affective memory*. Richard Boleslavsky made a very useful distinction between *affective memory*, as a *specific technique* for reviving and reliving a particular personal memory, and *emotion memory*, which is a much *wider* category - encompassing the actor's whole store of memories, experiences and impressions.

The American director, Charles Marowitz, has observed (in his book, *The Act of Being*) : "An actor is someone who remembers" - who recalls "what it felt like to be spurned, to be proud, to be angry, to be tender," and so on. "To be without memory and to be an actor is inconceivable."

Our own lives offer us a rich store of experiences, memories, observations and insights. "The broader your memory of emotions," Stanislavski argues, "the richer your material for inner creativity." But no one has sufficient material for all roles, so you must also observe other people closely. The actor needs "an infinitely broad point of view" to interpret different plays, and to create the life of people from different places and times.

Stanislavski suggests that the actor selects the "most absorbing memories" of feelings and sensations, and weaves the life of the character from them. But, as we've seen, he also recognised the danger in trying to force feelings too directly. He shows how subconscious memories and feelings can be indirectly evoked by different elements of the "system" - for example, belief in physical actions. The external elements of the production - lighting, sound, etc., - can also act as a stimulus and evoke living moods.

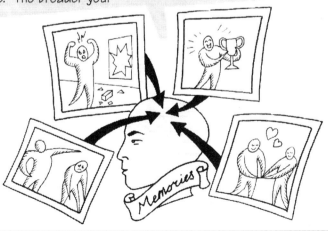

131

Communication (sometimes translated as "communion")

In life, we always speak with a purpose - to question, to explain, perhaps simply to pass the time. And we *listen* to each other because we are interested or need to hear something. To speak, in fact, is to act : to pursue an objective.

Actors often don't really *listen* to their partner in a scene ; they just switch off and wait for their next cue. It is very different when they really *communicate* - when

"one of them wants to convey his feelings to another, or to convince him of his ideas, and at the same time the other tries to take in those feelings and ideas."

Stanislavski always maintained that if actors really want to hold the attention of the audience, they must concentrate on maintaining an uninterrupted exchange of thoughts and feelings with other actors. To demonstrate this, he once drafted an imaginary conversation in an actor's dressing room, during the interval of a play:

If your feelings are conveyed to the other actors and affect them, you can rest assured that the spectator will be carried away, and not miss a single nuance of all you live through. However, if your feelings do not even reach your partner standing next to you, how do you expect them to reach the inattentive and noisy crowd of spectators, back in the twentieth row of the stalls?

Adaptation

We continually adjust or adapt to changes in circumstances. The time, the place, the weather - all make us adjust our behaviour. We also adapt, in infinitely subtle ways, to other people. If you are trying to achieve an *objective* - eg. to persuade someone to change their mind - then you try different strategies, and a variety of *adaptations*. If you see one strategy isn't working, you *adapt*, and try something new.

Unfortunately, actors often make their "adjustments" not to their partners in a scene, but to the audience, such as trying to make them laugh.

In 1927, Stanislavski worked on a production of a French melodrama called *The Sisters Gérard*. In one scene, Constable Picard is supposed to slip a sleeping potion into the drink of an old man, Martin. As an exercise, the scene was improvised, with Stanislavski taking the role of Picard. He tried all the ways he could devise to achieve his objective: to put the suspicious Martin to sleep. He offered him a pinch of snuff (drugged, of course)...

No, thank you, I don't take snuff.

So, he had to devise still more strategies. His focus throughout was on trying to achieve his objective; this made him adapt to the other person in the scene, moment by moment.

Inner motive forces of psychological life

Having discussed some of the major elements of the actor's psycho-technique, Stanislavski tries to define what he calls the "inner motive forces" which stir the actor's creativity.

They are, firstly, our feelings. Unfortunately feelings are elusive and cannot be forced. So, we use our mind, to initiate and activate our creativity. We also need to stir our will, our desire to create. The three elements always act together; they are inextricably linked. Take the improvisation with the madman at the door. The mind suggested the given circumstances, and stimulated both the feelings, and the will to do something.

The unbroken line

In every role, there must be a sense of continuous life, or as Stanislavski calls it, an *unbroken line*. If this line is broken, then it means the actor no longer understands what he or she is saying and doing - the life of the character stops.

In life, our attention switches from one thing to another - but we continue to live, think, breathe - so some sort of line continues.

Think through everything you have done today until now. What you will get is a series of different "episodes" or "short lines"; put them together and you have an extended line, the line of your life so far today.

Then think about what you're planning to do for the rest of the day.

Join this line with the former, and you will get one long, unbroken line of your life today - past, present, and future - from the moment of waking up in the morning until you go to sleep at night.

Now, if you were working, say, on the role of Othello, there would be one dominating idea in your life, that would absorb everything, leading up to the performance - an extended line stretching over several days and weeks.

Stanislavski goes further: "If there are lines running through days and weeks, can't there also be lines stretching over months and years - even a whole lifetime?"

The Superobjective

As you create your character's objectives, you can begin to get a sense of an overall goal, a line running through the play - a superobjective; e.g. :

"I want to kill the king..."

"I want to make her love me..."

When you have found the superobjective, it acts like a magnet. All the other objectives fall into place as steps leading to a final and all-embracing goal.

You can now trace an *extended line* running through the role, through all the steps the character takes to try to achieve their goal.

Stanislavski calls this the *"through line of action."*

The process of perezhivanie ("living through") consists in creating a "score" of the role, a superobjective, and its active attainment by means of the through line of action.

The "superobjective" and the "through line of action" are so important in the "system" that Stanislavski often regretted that he did not start the book with them. When he met Stella Adler in Paris, he asked her:

Do you know about the though line of action and the superobjective?

Yes, they told me something about that, but I did not understand it.

137

And yet, this is the crux of the whole system! Without it, "you are simply going through certain individual, disjointed exercises."

When an actor, then, has established the *superobjective*, all the "lines" of the role tend in one direction:

SUPER-
OBJECTIVE

But without it, the role is disjointed, and individual lines lead in different directions:

The "superobjective" of the play

Stanislavski also talks about the "superobjective," or *ruling idea*, running through a writer's work, and inspiring him or her to write. For example : Dostoevsky spent his whole life searching for the signs of God and the devil in people. The "search for God" is the ruling idea in *The Brothers Karamazov*. Tolstoy spent his life striving for self-perfection, and much of his writing was inspired by this idea. Anton Chekhov wrestled with the triviality and vulgarity of bourgeois society, and dreamed of a better life; and this became the *superobjective* of many of his stories and plays. It is important to define the ruling idea in a play. When Stanislavski was rehearsing Chekhov's *Three Sisters*, he felt the play at first wasn't coming to life. It seemed gloomy and dull. Then, suddenly, he realised what was missing.

Chekhov's characters do not wallow in their own sorrow. Just the opposite ; they seek joy, laughter, courage. They want to live and not to vegetate... I came to life, and intuitively knew what I had to do.

He had, it seems, discovered the "ruling idea" of the play: *the aspiration for a better life.*

An actor needs to keep the superobjective or ruling idea of the play in mind throughout the performance. It should penetrate, as deeply as possible, the actor's thoughts, feelings and imagination.

The characters' superobjectives need to be related to the "ruling idea" of the play. Thus, Chekhov's three sisters dream of going to Moscow, and escaping the triviality of provincial society; the *aspiration for a better life* is the ultimate goal they all share.

In 1913, Stanislavski played the role of Argan in Molière's comedy *The Imaginary Invalid*. At first, he decided that the character's superobjective was, "I want to be ill." But this made the play seem heavy; a satirical comedy was turning into a tragedy. Argan's superobjective was then redefined as: "I want to be thought ill."

Then the comic side immediately began to emerge, and the ground was prepared to show how the stupid Argan is exploited by the charlatans of the medical world - the very targets Molière wanted to ridicule in his play.

In other words, rethinking the *character's* superobjective helped to make the *play's* ruling idea clearer.

The subconscious

Tortsov's students are reaching the end of their first year of training. He reminds them that the goal of the "system" can be summed up in one phrase: the subconscious through the conscious.

When it became clear to Stanislavski that his book would be published in two volumes, he was concerned that the methods in the first volume, and the concept of "living through," might appear "ultra-naturalistic and the book will therefore be reviled."

Unfortunately, this has happened to a certain extent. It has been assumed by some that the methods are only suitable for "naturalistic" or "realistic" drama. Stanislavski argued that, in the early stages, an actor's work on a role has to be "realistic," even "ultra-naturalistic," because this "causes your subconscious to work and induces bursts of inspiration." But he wanted it made clear that the

purpose of the whole "system" is to lead to "superconscious creation."

When Kostya was asked to improvise a highly melodramatic scene, he was told to focus first on a small physical action - counting the money. The approach at this stage, then, was realistic, even "ultra-naturalistic"; it was designed to help the actor believe in the drama.

Now, Kostya is asked to improvise the scene again. This time he begins by relaxing and releasing physical tension. Then he thinks about the given circumstances, and asks himself: what would I do if I were in this situation? He becomes wholly absorbed in the action of the drama, and feels he is really living the role.

He again experiences "inspiration" on stage; but Tortsov points out that this time, it did not happen by chance; he "called for it," he prepared the way for it, through applying elements of the "system."

Stanislavski argued that his "system" is based on "nature's laws." The actor's natural creativity cannot be forced. The elements of the "system" are designed to create the conditions that help the actor to live on stage.

Kachalov once said that for the actor of the Art Theatre "every new role is the birth of a new person." Stanislavski himself often used the same image :

What is the aim of our art? It is the conception and birth of a new living being - the person in the part. It is a natural creative act, resembling the birth of a human being.

The aim is to achieve a transformation. As Shchepkin argued, you must turn yourself into the character, and "walk, talk, think, feel, cry, laugh," just as your character does.

Tortsov tells his students they have now acquired the basic elements of the actor's psycho-technique. However, the actor must also have a highly developed physical and vocal apparatus, sensitive to the slightest nuances and changes in our inner lives while on the stage.

The students' work, then, has only just begun...

THE ACTOR'S WORK ON THE SELF (Part Two)

The Transition to Physical Embodiment

Tortsov announces that the students' training will now concentrate on external, physical technique. They are set a simple exercise : they have to go onto the stage and bow before a woman, and kiss her hand. This seems easy enough; but the results are clumsy and laughable.

Most people don't know how to use their bodies - they have poor posture. On the stage, the actor is scrutinised as if under a magnifying glass; physical shortcomings are all too apparent and have to be eliminated. It is almost as if the actor has to learn to walk all over again.

Tortsov's students take lessons in gymnastics, acrobatics, dancing, etc.

- not only to correct errors, but also to develop movement that is fluid, clear and precise. The director reminds them, however, that on stage, no gesture must be made merely for its own sake : "Your actions must always have a purpose..."

Movement should not be seen simply as something external. In all movement, there is an *inner feeling* of energy passing through the body. There should be no "shreds and scraps of movement" on stage ; instead, you should aim for an *unbroken line* of movement, and an *uninterrupted flow* of energy.

Singing and diction

When Salvini was asked what you must have to be a tragedian he replied:

Voice, voice, and more voice!

Conventional forms of theatrical declamation had become hackneyed and false. Stanislavski stresses instead the need to start from the *inner sense* of the words and lines. However, this does *not* mean he wanted a *"naturalistic"* style of speech on stage.

Actors trained in the American "Method" have sometimes been accused of neglecting the importance of speech and mumbling their lines. But this would have horrified Stanislavski.

He wrote:

Speech is music. The text of a role or a play is the melody. The art of correct speech on the stage is as difficult as singing, it demands a training and technique bordering on virtuosity.

The careless pronunciation of words, letters and syllables is a mutilation of speech; it is like "having a flattened nose, or an eye or a tooth that has been knocked out."

The actor must combine the *meaning of* words, with an expressive use of the voice. A simple phrase like *"Come back! I cannot live without you!"* can be spoken in different ways, and with a variety of different meanings and moods.

How many possibilities there are in a word or a phrase! How rich language is! Its power lies, not in itself, but in the way it expresses the human soul, the human mind. So much is contained in those seven words: Come back, I cannot live without you - a whole human tragedy.

Speech and its Laws

Stanislavski stresses the importance of the *subtext*, which enables you to *feel* what lies beneath the words of the text. A play, in fact, is not a finished piece of work until it is acted on the stage and "brought to life by living human feelings."

Spectators come to the theatre to hear the subtext. They can read the text at home.

For a foreigner, for example, the word "love" is simply an empty sound. "But as soon as feelings, thoughts, imagination bring the empty sound to life, a different attitude is produced, the word becomes *meaningful*."

Words evoke images in our imagination. The word "love," for example, will bring a concrete image to your mind: a lover, a friend, etc. When you're describing something on stage, you need to *visualise* it in your imagination - and try to convey this picture to your partner; otherwise you are only saying the words. The actor, in fact, has to create an *unbroken line* of inner images, running parallel to the text - like "a moving picture, constantly passing over the screen of your inner vision." You must try to make your partner in a scene see what you see, and *feel* what lies behind the words - using all the means at your disposal, "every nuance of voice and movement."

The sphere of verbal action is tremendous. You can transmit thoughts simply by intonations, exclamations, words. The transmission of your thoughts is the action. Your thoughts, words, images - everything is done only for your partner.

Tortsov shows how a speech should be given a definite shape, with pauses, intonations and the accentuation of key words. He analyses a speech from "Othello" with great technical precision. But Kostya says: "In such moments, can actors be moved by such technical and professional calculations? What about inspiration?"

*Tortsov replies that the actor functions on **two levels** when acting. He quotes Salvini, who said...*

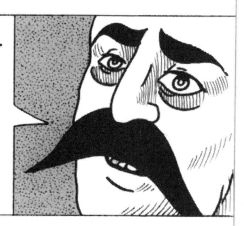

While I act, I live a double life. I laugh and cry and all the while I analyse my tears and laughter, in order to affect, all the stronger, the hearts of the people I want to move.

When you are acting, you do not forget for one minute that you are on a stage. (Stanislavski argued that "actors who say that they immerse themselves so completely in their roles that they do not remember anything, they are so overwhelmed by emotions, are just making hysterical remarks.") One half of the actor's soul during a performance is absorbed by the superobjective, the subtext, "the elements which go to make up the inner creative state." But the other half operates as an observer, monitoring the performance on a more technical level. This does not prevent you living the role; it "does not harm inspiration. On the contrary! The one helps the other."

Put it another way: there are two perspectives...

One is the **perspective of the character**
The other is the **perspective of the actor**

Your *own* perspective, as the actor playing the role, is necessary so that at every given moment on stage you can watch for any problems, such as muscular tension. You can sustain your concentration and focus on your objectives. Perspective also means you can see your role as a *whole*. You can see how it develops through the course of the play - and pace your performance accordingly. Salvini as Othello, for example, "always knew the line of perspective of the play, beginning with the outbursts of youthful, passionate love, on his first entrance, and ending with the supreme hatred of a jealous killer at the conclusion of the tragedy. With mathematical precision and inexorable logic, point by point, he plotted in his soul the evolution of the entire role."

The notion of *perspective* bears a close resemblance to the *through line of action*. They are not identical - but they run in parallel.

Tempo-rhythm

As we have seen, there is a tempo and rhythm in everything we do - both internal and external.

Tempo denotes the speed of an action. Every act takes time. When you accelerate the tempo, you give yourself less time and so you have to perform and speak more quickly.

Rhythm comes not only from changes in speed, but also with stress. If for example, in a steady tempo, you stress every second beat of the metronome, you get march time; if you stress every third beat, you get a waltz.

Tortsov says that if you haven't felt tempo-rhythm in your own body, then scientific definitions can't help you. They will only prevent you from freely enjoying rhythm on the stage and playing with it like a toy. The students experiment in clapping in different tempi and rhythms. This produces "the most contrasting moods," from "andante maestoso" to "allegro vivace."

Next, Tortsov sets an improvisation, in which the students have to act and move in a given tempo-rhythm. He asks them to imagine setting out on a train journey: queuing for a ticket, browsing through the bookstall, etc. These actions are at first executed calmly, because there is plenty of time before the train is scheduled to leave.

Then, they repeat the exercise - and this time they have only a quarter of an hour to get everything ready - and there's a long queue at the ticket office... Kostya says: "This was enough to make my heart beat faster - especially as I suffer from travel sickness."

There is, then, a new "tempo-rhythm" - one full of agitation and hurry. The exercise is repeated once more, and this time Tortsov tells them : "You arrive at the station at the very last minute !" The result is a sense of great haste and alarm.

A change in the *given circumstances*, then, produces a change in tempo-rhythm ; the two are always closely related.

The change in tempo-rhythm affects the actors' mood. There is a close connection between rhythm and feeling. Try any action - walking, sitting down, getting dressed - in any conceivable tempo and rhythm, and you will find "that you will remember, receive and recognise the most varied inner feelings and sensations."

There is tempo-rhythm in speech as well as in movement. The rhythm of the text "must live in the actor, both when he is speaking, and when he is silent. The whole production must be charged with rhythm even in the pauses between words and sentences. They should all fall into the necessary rhythm."

Logic and sequence

Stanislavski argues that in real life our actions are logical and sequential, because our actions in life are really necessary for us. On the stage, we forget the logic even in the smallest action. For example : if in real life you want to drink a glass of water, first you must take the top off the carafe, then put the glass under it, tilt the bottle and pour. If you pour the water without holding the glass underneath, then the result is a bit of a mess ...

But on stage, the simplest actions are sometimes performed carelessly, without the requisite attention to logic and sequence.

Again, you have to reflect on how you would do something in real life; you have to ask yourself, what would I do if I was in this situation? You should answer this question, not in words, but in concrete physical action.

Stanislavski stresses that logic and sequentiality are particularly important in portraying feelings. You cannot grasp a passion such as love at one stroke. You have to create a chain of internal and external actions. What does someone do when they fall in love ? The feeling develops in logical stages. First, the couple meet. They are attracted to each other; they find pretexts for another meeting... Later: the first kiss. They make growing demands on each other. One of them becomes jealous. There's a break, followed by forgiveness and reconciliation. And so on.

Stanislavski suggests that if you carry out each step in this series of concrete actions ; if you put yourself in the situation, imagining all the circumstances in detail - then the feeling will follow.

Actors who try to embrace an emotion all at once fall into generalisation. Truth is concrete, and generalisation is the enemy of art.

Characterisation

How do you find the physical form and image of the character? Stanislavski suggests that this sometimes happen intuitively - once the character's inner life has been established. He cites his own experience when playing Dr. Stockman. Premature anxiety about the physical characterisation, in fact, can lead the actor to imitation, and this can hinder and even immobilise the development of a living character.

Stanislavski warns against finding the characterisation simply through external tricks like adopting a squint or a limp, but he then reflects that the external affects the internal; assuming a different physical form can cause an almost imperceptible internal change. But you must work from accurate observation and not from stereotypes or clichés. If you are playing an elderly person, and you carefully and accurately develop the character's physical life, this will also influence your sense of the inner life.

The actor might take the external image from observation, from the experience of daily life, from pictures, books, etc.

In all your research into external form, the only proviso is that you must not lose your inner self.

Tortsov announces that the students must dress up in costume and create a character for a "masquerade." Kostya plays a venomous critic. He begins to find movement and gestures quite intuitively. Finally when he sees himself in make-up he declares : "It's him !" He becomes transformed into the character. Yet, he never loses the sense of being himself. Part of him continues to observe his own performance.

He is playing someone quite different from himself - and yet, he reflects, at the end of the day, the character "was taken from my own nature." The feelings he experienced were his own.

Ultimately, you can only draw on yourself in creating a character - on your own emotional and physical resources. However, to play "from yourself" does not mean simply "be yourself" on stage. In each part, you recreate yourself in a unique new form.

Stanislavski attacks actors who use the stage simply to show off their own personalities, or their good looks - actors who love themselves in the part more than the part in them. "There is a great difference between searching in yourself and choosing emotions related to a role, and adapting the role to suit your own personality."

Self-control and finish

Tortsov's students repeat the improvisation with the madman at the door. They play with belief and commitment, but Tortsov says this is not enough. The problem is that their performances are too **naturalistic**.

Superfluous gestures only clutter a performance. The aim is not to reproduce life in all its detail, like a photographer, but to select the essential. Only then can you achieve the necessary clarity and precision.

Stanislavski, then, does not want "naturalistic" movement. Someone who is carried away by emotion in real life is "incapable of talking about it at the same time, because tears choke him, his voice breaks, and the agitation makes his thoughts confused." But the actor is not carried away with emotion in this way. For one thing, you know the situation is not actually real. Stanislavski makes it clear he is looking, not for raw emotion, but emotion "recollected in tranquillity." It is like telling the story of a tragedy you have experienced. In telling the story, you recall the emotions you felt, but at the same time, you stay relatively calm - while your audience weeps ...

You are, moreover, always able to *observe* your own performance - and so control the way you express the feelings. The actor needs a certain restraint and control in portraying emotion. Stanislavski once commented that a certain actor in the Art Theatre could "shed tears easily," but he was more effective when he held the emotion in check - at those moments when "the tears begin to come" but "he does not give way."

Ethics and Discipline

Stanislavski stresses the importance of ethics in the theatre. You need to see yourself as part of an *ensemble*, where everyone must work together, in a disciplined way, to create the right conditions for artistic work. He says :

Never come into the theatre with mud on your feet. Shake off all the dust and dirt outside. Leave your overshoes in the cloakroom - and with them all your little worries, quarrels and troubles - all the things that make your life difficult, and take your attention away from your art.

LEAVE YOUR WORRIES ON THE DOORSTEP

The Bases of the "System"

Tortsov acknowledges that the students are probably still rather confused in their minds about all the different elements of the "system"; and so he suggests they prepare a chart, putting the elements into some sort of sequence and order.

The result looks something like this:

THE SUBCONSCIOUS

GENERAL CREATIVE STATE

INNER CREATIVE STATE

EXTERNAL CREATIVE STATE

INNER HABIT AND TRAINING

EXTERNAL HABIT AND TRAINING

THE ELEMENTS OF THE INNER CREATIVE STATE

(Imagination, 'as if', given circumstances, concentration, units, objectives, etc.)

THE ELEMENTS OF THE EXTERNAL CREATIVE STATE

(voice, speech, tempo-rythm, self-control & finish, etc.)

THE INNER MOTIVE FORCES OF OUR PSYCHOLOGICAL LIFE

MIND

WILL

FEELING

THE PROCESS OF LIVING THROUGH

RELAXATION OF MUSCLES

THE PROCESS OF PHYSICAL EMBODIMENT

THE FUNDAMENTAL PRINCIPLES OF THE SYSTEM

The art of the actor is the art of internal and external action

Feelings that seem true in the given circumstances

The subconscious through the conscious

The goal of art: the creation of the spiritual life of the role

THE ACTOR'S WORK ON THE SELF

The two sides of the chart - the process of living through, and the process of physical embodiment - are equally important.

The state of physical readiness, when the actor's whole body is poised for action, is called the "external creative state."

When this is combined with the *inner creative state*, the actor achieves the *general* or *overall creative state*. When you are in this condition, "every inner feeling, every mood, every experience is expressed reflexively" in the body.

The actor must try to maintain this general creative state in all creative work - in rehearsal and in performance. "Without it, you cannot grasp your role. It must become second nature for every one of us - a normal, natural, organic condition."

The elements of the "system" are interdependent. A lack of concentration, or muscular tension, for example, affects all the other elements.

The "system" may seem complex and difficult to master. (Kostya himself says : "Good God, how difficult and complicated it is ! We'll never take it all in !") But Stanislavski emphasises the need for continual practice and training, until "the difficult becomes habitual ; the habitual, easy ; the easy, beautiful."

The "system" is not a cook book, where all you need to prepare a dish is to look in the index, find the page and there is your recipe. No, it is not so simple. The "system" is not a reference book, but a whole way of life ...

Act VII: The Last Act

Stanislavski continued working on his book for a number of years. The first part was published in Russia in 1938, but he did not live to see it. An advance copy was sent to his house just three weeks after his death ...

While convalescing in Nice, he was also drafting a plan for a production of *Othello*, which he sent in instalments to the theatre. It was very different from his earlier production plans; it included suggestions on staging, but he was far more concerned with guiding the actors' work - using elements of the "system." He broke scenes down, for example, into units, and defined the objectives and actions of the characters.

Above all he wanted to help Leonid Leonidov, who was cast as Othello, by creating a "score" of the role which was clear and logical, and based in the simplest physical actions. "A complicated psychological line with all its subtleties and nuances," Stanislavski wrote, "will only confuse you."

The play was rushed into production, to fill a gap in the schedules. It was directed by Ilya Sudakov. Leonidov said Stanislavski's production plan was "a masterpiece of the art of directing, but unfortunately it is hard to put it into practice when you are working at such speed." To make matters worse, the actor was suffering from acute agoraphobia, and sometimes had to cling to furniture on stage for support; his performance, which was promising in rehearsal, seemed to fall apart during the previews.

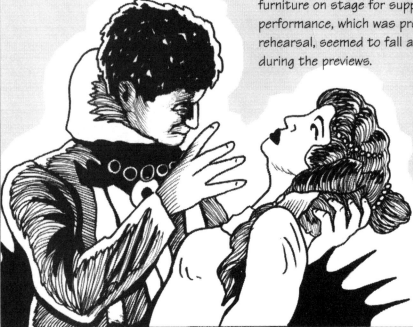

The production lasted for onl eighteen performances

156

According to some Western newspapers, Stanislavski had decided he could no longer work in Russia under the communists. But he was bemused by these reports, and declared, "How could I not return?" He arrived back in Moscow on 3 November 1930.

He discovered that things had changed for the worse. In 1929, a communist official, a so-called "red director," had been appointed to manage the Art Theatre alongside Stanislavski and Nemirovich. Pressure was now being put on the company to stage more plays and to perform more often. This was in tune with the emphasis on output and mass production in Stalin's first Five-Year Plan. It meant, for example, that in the 1930-31 season, there were 750 performances in just 260 days.

Stanislavski was alarmed by the new emphasis on "breadth" rather than "depth," and by the way the theatre was being forced to stage primitive propaganda plays. He wrote directly to Stalin, arguing that art could not grow by bureaucratic interference and directives. The result was the "red director" was removed, and the Theatre was taken under direct government control ; it became the Moscow Art Academic Theatre of the USSR.

The company at first experienced some return of artistic autonomy, but in future years, there would be a heavy price to pay...

In 1934 all Soviet writers were united in a single union and were forced to adopt a single style, **"Socialist Realism."** All art, it was decreed, should be **"realistic,"** and offer a positive picture of life under Socialism. Experimental art was labelled **"formalist"** - the ultimate term of abuse at the time (implying a concern with external form, and a lack of inner content). Much of the most innovative theatre work in recent years, such as Meyerhold's, was condemned in this way.

Stanislavski seemed to welcome the turn against "formalism," evidently believing that it arose from the government's concern for true art. But did he really know what was happening in the country? Did he even know what was happening in his own theatre?

His health was still precarious. After 1934, he never entered the Art Theatre again. He worked from home, in Leontyevski Lane - hermetically sealed from the weather to protect him from colds ; and sealed from the outside world, and the political realities of the last years of his life.

In 1936, Stalin began the physical liquidation of all those who might oppose his dictatorship. Moscow witnessed the infamous "show trials." Members of the Art Theatre were now expected to offer their "unanimous" support to the execution of military leaders or "subversives," and make speeches supporting Stalin's atrocities. A number of other theatres were closed. In 1938, Meyerhold's Theatre was dissolved. It was branded a "class-alien" establishment, distinguished by a "systematic deviation from Soviet reality, political distortion of that reality, and hostile slanders against our way of life." The Art Theatre company drew up a statement welcoming this development. But Stanislavski surprised everyone by inviting Meyerhold to work with him, first

as a teacher in the new Opera-Drama Studio and then as director at the Stanislavski Opera Theatre. When people objected, he told them : "Meyerhold is needed in the theatre." He accepted full responsibility for the decision. It was a bold move - offering protection to someone in Stalin's disfavour.

A few weeks before his death, Stanislavski said to the Opera Theatre's production manager, Yuri Bakhruschin :

Take care of Meyerhold. He is my only heir in the theatre - not only in our theatre, but also in general.

Stanislavski's goal in his final years, his *superobjective*, was to teach, to communicate his discoveries about acting. As he told one group of actors:

Laurels for directing do not interest me now. Whether I stage one production more or less does not matter. It is important to me to hand on to you everything I have accumulated throughout my life.

Bulgakov's play, *Molière*, had been accepted for production in 1931; rehearsals began in 1932, under Nikolai Gorchakov. Then Stanislavski fell ill again, and was forced to go abroad; the production was put on hold. He finally saw a run-through in March 1935. He said the play failed to communicate a sense of Molière's greatness, and pressure was put on Bulgakov to rewrite it. Meanwhile, the date of the opening was put off indefinitely...

Every rehearsal with Stanislavski became a master class in the "system." He could be extremely demanding; his favourite phrase was, "I don't believe it..." The actors found the process "exhausting, sometimes agonising." Stanislavski, meanwhile, feared he wasn't getting through to them - once more encountering resistance to his methods. He told them:

I still haven't found the way to your hearts, but when you understand it, you will be astonished at how simple it all is.

Eventually the production was taken out of his hands by the Theatre's Board of Management. We do not know his reaction...

The play finally opened in February 1936. Again, Bulgakov was the target of the critics' wrath. Then the Chairman of the State Committee for the Arts, Pyotr Kerzhentsev, wrote to Stalin, describing play as an attempt to draw a parallel between Molière's position under the tyranny of Louis XIV, and the position of a writer under communism. He said the theatre should be made to realise that it had strayed from "the line of socialist realism." Stalin responded: "I think Comrade Kerzhentsev is right."

Shortly afterwards, Bulgakov left the Art Theatre. He went on to write a novel, "Black Snow," based on his experiences; it is a thinly disguised satire on Stanislavski ...

In 1936, Stanislavski assembled a small group of actors from the Art Theatre to work on Molière's Tartuffe. The plan was not to prepare the play for production but to focus on acting technique - in particular, a new way of working on a role, which Stanislavski termed *The Method of Physical Actions*.

REHEARSING 'TARTUFFE'

Traditionally, rehearsals in the Art Theatre had begun with a series of discussions around a table, exploring and analysing the play. (For *Hamlet* alone, there were 159 rehearsals "around the table.") But Stanislavski feared this process only cluttered the actor's mind with too much information. He wanted to find a practical method which would get the actors on their feet early on in rehearsals, so they could begin to experience the role physically.

Stanislavski considered the Method of Physical Actions to be the culmination of his life's work. It is described in his notes for his unfinished book, *The Actor's Work on the Role* (a kind of sequel to *The Actor's Work on the Self ...*). Again, the form is a fictional "diary" written by the drama student, Kostya...

Tortsov announces to his students : "Here is my approach to a new role. Without any preliminary read-through of the new play, without any discussions about it, the actors are asked to come to the first rehearsal." The students demand : "How is that possible?"

"You don't believe me?" he answers. "Let's put it to the test..." Kostya is asked to start performing a scene from Gogol's "The Government Inspector." He objects that he has only a rough recollection of the play : "I can't do anything because I don't know anything." "What ?!" Tortsov protests. "In the play it says: 'Enter Khlestakov.' Don't you know how to go into a room in an inn?"

"I do."

"Well, do it ..."

The work begins with a simple physical task. But even a simple task such as entering a room can be difficult for the actor on stage. It must be performed logically and precisely. Moreover, you cannot simply enter a room, without thinking about the given circumstances. In order to come on stage "like a human being and not like an actor," you have to find out "who you are, what has happened to you, under what conditions you are living here, how you spend your day," and so on.

The Method of Physical Actions immediately puts you in the middle of the *given circumstances*. It makes you ask yourself: what would you *do* if you were in this situation? You experience the situation as you perform the actions. You begin, in some small way, to *feel yourself in the part*. Entering a room, moreover, immediately evokes the question: what is your objective?

Why do you want to enter the room ?

When Stanislavski talks about *physical action*, he does not, in fact, mean simple, mechanical tasks, such as opening a door. Rather, he means action directed towards the *achievement of an objective*.

Tortsov divides the scene from "The Government Inspector" into a series of three physical actions: the central character, Khlestakov, enters the room; he scolds his manservant, Osip, for lounging around on the bed; then, he wants to make Osip go out and try to get some food.

Each scene in a play can be broken down into four or five physical actions, in this way.

Stanislavski advises actors to work through the whole play and...

... build the simplest scheme of physical actions of the role. Follow the unbroken line of these actions, and you will have already achieved at least thirty-five percent of the role.

Creating the physical life of the role, however, "is only the beginning" of the work: "The most important part lies ahead. We must deepen this life until it reaches the very depths, where the life of the human spirit begins." Working from physical actions stimulates the actor to explore the character's inner life. Now there is a real need to analyse and investigate the given circumstances, the character's objectives, and so on, in more depth.

To some extent, Stanislavski was now working from the outer to the inner, from the physical to the spiritual. He recognised that physical actions are more accessible and tangible than feelings. But as we have seen, every action has a psychological element. Starting with physical actions, and executing them logically, the actor begins to penetrate the inner life of the role, and live through "the deepest and most complicated feelings and emotional experiences."

The new method did not annul or replace any other elements of the "system." In fact, it was a way of trying to bring the different elements together, and giving them a concrete basis. Physical actions became the "frame" on which the actor could build the performance.

1938 - forty years since the opening of the Moscow Art Theatre... The two co-founders had not spoken to each other for a number of years, but in February, the death of Nemirovich's wife prompted Stanislavski to write:

There have been many misunderstandings between us in recent years, damaging our good relationship ... I want to say to you, as a friend, that I feel for you sincerely and profoundly and am looking for ways to help you. *Stanislavski*

Nemirovich replied, blaming their strained relationship on differences in temperament, and artistic methods - and jealous meddling by other people.

Our relationship has lasted 41 years. A historian, some theatrical Nestor, not lacking in humour, will say: "Just imagine! These people - they themselves and the people round them - tried to destroy this relationship, and fought over it - and yet, history has shown that it could not be destroyed..." *Nemirovich*

All the same, they never met again. On 2 August, Stanislavski was preparing to travel to a sanatorium. But his temperature was 39.2.°, and his pulse was weak. There was no question of going anywhere. On the morning of the 7th, he seemed to get better and was even talking a little. He told the doctors that he was not ill, only exhausted. Suddenly he said:

And who is looking after Nemirovich now?... Is he ill, perhaps? Is he short o money?

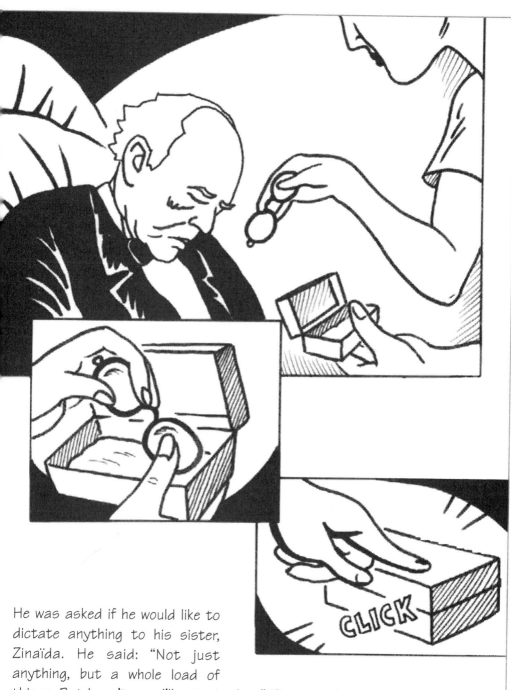

He was asked if he would like to dictate anything to his sister, Zinaïda. He said: "Not just anything, but a whole load of things. But I can't now, I'll get mixed up." They were his last words. At 3.45, the nurse came to take his temperature, but he suddenly shuddered, as if from fear. He became deathly pale, and his head dropped forward. He had stopped breathing.

He was buried in the Novodyevichi Cemetery, next to Chekhov and Simov. The actors who had been working on *Tartuffe* decided to carry on his work, and stage a full production of the play. It opened on 4 December 1939.

In June 1939, Meyerhold was arrested. He was shot in prison on 2 February 1940.

2067   MEYERHOLD

By the time of Stanislavski's death, the Moscow Art Theatre had become the official model for all theatres in the Soviet Union. Soviet critics subsequently attempted to marginalise his experiments in different styles (such as symbolism) and see him as the great progenitor of Socialist Realism. **The "system"** was the approved curriculum in every theatrical institute. His ideas, then, which he always saw as exploratory and developmental, were fossilised and turned into official dogma.

Stanislavski believed that the art of the theatre demands "constant renewal, constant, persistent work ... It is alive, and like everything living, it must have uninterrupted development and movement."

Such an art demands a special technique - not a technique of fixed methods, but a technique for mastering the natural laws of human creativity - and with it, the ability to influence this nature, to control it, to discover at every performance your own creative possibilities, your own intuition.

The "system" cannot make you a great actor. It should not be seen as an end in itself. It is an aid, "a companion on the way to creative achievement."

My system should serve as a kind of door to creativity - but you must be able to open the door for yourself ...

My Life in Art was first published in English in 1924.
The Actor's Work on the Self was first published in two volumes as *An Actor Prepares* (1936) and *Building a Character* (1950).
The Actor's Work on the Role was published as *Creating a Role* (1961).
A collection of Stanislavski's essays and notes appeared as *Stanislavski's Legacy* in 1958.
These translations are widely regarded as unreliable. Fortunately, a new Collected Works is now being published.

Also recommended :

Stanislavski : An Introduction by Jean Benedetti (1982)
Stanislavski : A Biography by Jean Benedetti (1988)
The Moscow Art Theatre Letters by Jean Benedetti (1991)
Stanislavski and the Actor by Jean Benedetti (1998)
Black Snow by Mikhail Bulgakov (1967)
Stanislavski Directs by Nikolai Gorchakov (1985)
The Stanislavski Technique : Russia by Mel Gordon (1987)
Stanislavski's Encounter with Shakespeare : The Evolution of a Method by Joyce Vining Morgan (1984)
Gordon Craig's Moscow "Hamlet" : A Reconstruction by Laurence Senelick (1982)
Is Comrade Bulgakov Dead ? : Mikhail Bulgakov at the Moscow Art Theatre by Anatoly Smeliansky (1993)
Stanislavski Produces "Othello" by Constantin Stanislavski (1948)
Stanislavski on Opera by Constantin Stanislavski and Pavel Rumyantsev (1975)
Stanislavski in Rehearsal : The Final Years by Vasily Toporkov (1979)
The Moscow Art Theatre by Nick Worrall (1996)

Sources

Quotations have been taken from the following sources : K.S. Stanislavski, *Sobranie sochineni*, 8 vols (Moscow: 1951-64) ; *Sobranie sochineni*, 7 vols (of 9) (Moscow: 1988-95) ; *Rezhisserski plan "Otello"* (Moscow: 1945) ; *Rezhisserskie eksemplyari K.S. Stanislavskogo*, 5 vols (of 6) (Moscow: 1980-88) and : Günter Ahrends, *Konstantin Stanislawski : Neue Aspekte und Perspektiven* (Tübingen: 1992) ; N. Balatova and A. Svobodin, *"Sistema" K.S.*

Stanislavskogo : slovar' terminov (Moscow : 1994) ; Martha Bradshaw, ed., *Soviet Theaters 1917 - 1941* (New York: 1954) ; Edward Braun, *The Theatre of Meyerhold* (London : 1986) ; Valeri Bryusov, *Sobranie sochineni*, Vol. 6 (Moscow: 1975) ; Harold Clurman, *The Fervent Years* (New York: 1975) ; Toby Cole, ed., *Acting : A Handbook of the Stanislavski Method* (New York : 1955) ; Christine Edwards, *The Stanislavsky Heritage* (London : 1966) ; T.M. El'nitskaya and O.M. Fel'dman, *Mikhail Semenovich Shchepkin : zhizn' i tvorchestvo*, Vol. 1 (Moscow : 1984) ; Aleksandr Gladkov, *Meyerhol'd*, 2 vols (Moscow : 1990) ; N. Gorchakov, *Rezhisserskie uroki Vakhtangova* (Moscow : 1957) ; Foster Hirsch, *A Method to Their Madness : The History of the Actors Studio* (New York: 1984) ; Alma Law, *An "Actor's Director" Debuts in the West* (interview with Tovstonogov) in *American Theatre*, June 1987 ; Charles Marowitz, *The Act of Being* (London : 1978) ; V.I. Nemirovich-Danchenko, *Rozhdenie teatra* (Moscow : 1989) ; E. Polyakova, *Stanislavski* (Moscow : 1977) ; J.W. Roberts, *Richard Boleslavsky : His Life and Work in the Theatre* (Ann Arbor, Michigan : 1981) ; K. Rudnitski, *Meyerhol'd* (Moscow : 1981) ; Laurence Senelick, *Gordon Craig's Moscow "Hamlet" : A Reconstruction* (Westport, Connecticut : 1982) ; Anatoli Smelyanski, *Mikhail Bulgakov v Khudozhestvennom teatre* (Moscow : 1989) ; Constantin Stanislavski and Pavel Rumyantsev, *Stanislavski on Opera* (New York : 1975) ; M.N. Stroeva, *Rezhisserskie iskaniya Stanislavskogo 1917 - 1938* (Moscow : 1977) ; E.D. Surkov, ed., *Chekhov i teatr* (Moscow : 1961) ; V. Toporkov, *K.S. Stanislavski na repetitsii* (Moscow : 1950) ;, ed., *Vstrechi s Meyerhol'dom* (Moscow : 1967) ; V. Vilenkin, ed. L.D. Bendrovskaya, *Ol'ga Leonardovna Knipper-Chekhova*, 2 vols (Moscow : 1972) ; I. Vinogradskaya, *Zhizn' i tvorchestvo K.S. Stanislavskogo : Letopis'*, 4 vols (Moscow : 1971-76) ; Nick Worrall, *The Moscow Art Theatre* (London : 1996). Thanks to my wife, Ol'ga, for her help and advice on translating material from Russian. DAA, 1999.

Index

GESTALT FOR BEGINNERS ™
Sergio Sinay
Illustrated by Pable Blasberg
Translated by Mariana Solanet
ISBN 0-86316-258-4
(UK £7.99)

The origins of Gestalt Therapy derive from several sources, such as psychoanalysis by way of Wilhelm Reich and experimental Gestalt psychologists studying the nature of visual perception. It also includes field theorists such as Lewin and Humanist-Existential ideas that come primarily through the work of philosopher Martin Buber.

Gestalt, a German word with no exact equivalent in English, is usually translated as *form* or *shape*. Gestalt Therapy takes an holistic approach to healing and personal growth. It is a form of experiential psychology that focuses on elements of the *here* and *now*. What we experience as we develop and how we adapt to that experience, come into the present as unresolved problems.

The purpose of Gestalt therapy is to teac people to work through and complete unresolved problems. Clients learn to follow their own ongoing process and to fully experience, accept and appreciate their complete selves.

Gestalt For Beginners ™ details the birt of the therapy, investigates the complex life of its creator Fitz Peris, and describes his revolutionary techniques such as the **Empty Chair**, the **Monodrama**, and the **Dream Studies**. The author also demonstrates why Gestalt Therapy is an ideal approach to self-affirmation and personal growth.

SAI BABA FOR BEGINNERS ™
Marcelo Berenstein
Illustrated by Miguel Angel
Scenna
Translated by Mariana
Solanet
ISBN 0-86316-257-6
(UK £7.99)

120million devotees worldwide recognise Sathya Sai Baba as a modern Hindu *avatr* (a human incarnation of the dicine) with the ability to be in various places simultaneously and with absolute knbowledge.

Why does this man claim to be God? Who gave him that title? And what did he come here for? **Sai Baba For Beginners** ™

details Sai Baba's life from his birth in 1926 to his studies, miracles, works, programme of education in human valo and his messages, up to the celebration his recent 70th Birthday.

**HIGH PAVEMENT
COLLEGE LIBRARY**

september 1998

THE HISTORY OF
CINEMA FOR
BEGINNERS ™
Jarek Kupść
N 0-86316-275-4
(UK £9.99)

The History of Cinema for Beginners™ is an informative introductory text on the history of narrative film and a reference guide for those who seek basic information on interesting movies. The book spans over one hundred years of film history, beginning with events leading up to the invention of the medium and chronicles the early struggle of the pioneers.

Readers are introduced to people behind and in front of the camera and presented with all major achievements of the silent and sound periods - even the most intangible film theories are explained and made easily digestible.

The unique aspect of **The History of Cinema For Beginners™** is its global approach to the subject of film history. The author introduces the reader to such significant developments as the Soviet montage, Italian neorealism, the French New Wave, the British kitchen sink cinema and the New German Film while providing a comprehensive coverage of American genre films such as slapstick comedy, the western, film noir, and science-fiction.

In addition, **The History of Cinema For Beginners™** invites the reader to delve into the lesser known regions of World cinema: Eastern Europe, South-East Asia, South America and others. The book also presents every key figure in the vast world of cinema with detailed information on his or her background, technique and major accomplishments. In a lighthearted manner, film makers such as D.W. Griffiths, Sergei Eisenstein and Orson Welles present their unique approach to movie making. The book's main goal is to make learning about movies as entertaining as it is watching them.

MODERNISM FOR
BEGINNERS ™
Jim Powell
strated by Joe Lee
N 0-86316-139-1
(U.K. £7.99)

If you are like most people, you're not sure what Postmodernism is. And if this were like most books on the subject, it probably wouldn't tell you.

Besides what a few grumpy critics claim, Postmodernism is not a bunch of meaningless intellectual mind games. On the contrary, it is a reaction to the most profound spiritual and philosophical crises of our time -- the failure of the Enlightenment.

Jim Powell takes the position that Postmodernism is a series of *maps* that help people find their way through a changing world. **Postmodernism For Beginners**™ features the thoughts of Foucault on power and knowledge, Jameson on mapping the postmodern, Baudrillard on the media, Harvey on time-space compression, Derrida on deconstruction, and Deleuze and Guattari on rhizomes. The book also discusses postmodern artifacts such as Madonna, cyberpunk sci-fi, Buddhist ecology and teledildonics.

accept **no** substitute!

> Great ideas and great thinkers can be thrilling. They can also be intimidating

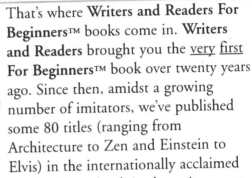

That's where **Writers and Readers For Beginners**™ books come in. **Writers and Readers** brought you the <u>very</u> <u>first</u> **For Beginners**™ book over twenty years ago. Since then, amidst a growing number of imitators, we've published some 80 titles (ranging from Architecture to Zen and Einstein to Elvis) in the internationally acclaimed **For Beginners**™ series. Every book in the series serves one purpose: to UNintimidate and UNcomplicate the works of the great thinkers. Knowledge is too important to be confined to the experts.

And Knowledge as you will discover in our **Documentary Comic Books**, is fun! Each book is painstakingly researched, humorously written and illustrated in whatever style best suits the subject at hand. That's where **Writers and Readers, For Beginners**™ books began! Remember if it doesn't say...

Writers and Readers

...it's not an original For Beginners book.